ELIZABETHAN PARLIAMENTS
1559–1601

Elizabethan Parliaments 1559–1601
SECOND EDITION

MICHAEL A. R. GRAVES

LONGMAN
LONDON AND NEW YORK

Pearson Education Limited
Edinburgh Gate,
Harlow, Essex CM20 2JE,
United Kingdom
and Associated Companies throughout the world

Visit us on the World Wide Web at:
http://www.pearsoneduc.com

©Addison Wesley Longman Limited 1987, 1996
The right of Michael A. R. Graves to be
identified as author of this work has been
asserted by him in accordance with the
Copyright, Designs and Patents Act 1988.

First published 1987
Second edition 1996

ISBN 0 582 291968

British Library Cataloguing in Publication Data

A catalogue record for this book is available from the British Library

Library of Congress Cataloging-in-Publication Data

Graves, Michael A. R.
Elizabethan parliaments, 1559-1601 / Michael A.R. Graves. -- 2nd ed.
    p.   cm. -- (Seminar studies in history)
Includes bibliographical references and index.
ISBN 0-582-29196-8
1. Great Britain. Parliament--History--16th century. 2. Great Britain--Politics and
government--1558-1603. I. Title. II. Series
JN525.G73   1996
328.42'09'031--dc20   96-10366
                                                                        CIP

7 6 5 4 3
06 05 04 03 02

Set in Sabon
Printed in Malaysia, CLP

CONTENTS

EDITORIAL FOREWORD

Such is the pace of historical enquiry in the modern world that there is an ever-widening gap between the specialist article or monograph, incorporating the results of current research, and general surveys, which inevitably become out of date. *Seminar Studies in History* are designed to bridge this gap. The books are written by experts in their field who are not only familiar with the latest research but have often contributed to it. They are frequently revised, in order to take account of new information and interpretations. They provide a selection of documents to illustrate major themes and provoke discussion, and also a guide to further reading. Their aim is to clarify complex issues without over-simplifying them, and to stimulate readers into deepening their knowledge and understanding of major themes and topics.

ROGER LOCKYER

NOTE ON REFERENCING SYSTEM

Readers should note that numbers in square brackets [5] refer them to the corresponding entry in the Bibliography at the end of the book (specific page numbers are given in italics). A number in square brackets preceded by *Doc.* [*Doc. 5*] refers readers to the corresponding item in the Documents section which follows the main text.

ACKNOWLEDGEMENTS

The publishers would like to thank the following for permission to reproduce copyright material: Cambridge University Press for several extracts from *De Republica Anglorum*, by Sir Thomas Smith, edited by M. Dewar, 1982; an extract from *Proceedings in the Parliaments of Elizabeth I*, by T.E. Hartley, 1981 by permission of Leicester University Press (a Cassell imprint), London. All rights reserved; Her Majesty's Stationery Office for an extract from The Journal of Commons' Proceedings, 1572, by Fulk Onslow, *The Historical Manuscripts Commission Reports*, The Manuscripts of the House of Lords, Vol. xi, addenda 1514–1714.

PART ONE: BACKGROUND

1 PRE-TUDOR PARLIAMENTS

When Henry Tudor became King of England in 1485 representative assemblies existed in France, the various Spanish kingdoms, the Holy Roman Empire, the Low Countries, Sicily and Poland, indeed in most European countries. They varied in age – some being older than the English parliaments – in authority and in the frequency of their meetings. However, they had one common characteristic. Their structure reflected the formal division of society into three estates of clergy, nobility and the rest. In practice, parliamentary power, especially the power to resist the monarch's financial demands, was usually confined to the first two estates, whilst, in some cases, representation of the third estate had become restricted to the towns. Nevertheless, most continental assemblies consisted of competing social orders which sat apart and deliberated separately. English parliaments, however, evolved in a quite different way. They had begun as meetings of the King and his professional counsel with his great council of spiritual and temporal magnates, in order to treat of important matters of government. As such, they embodied a basic medieval principle of government by consent of the community and they expressed a sense of unity and consensus. Sometimes, therefore, parliaments included shire (county) and borough (town) representatives, whose prime function was to grant taxes in response to royal requests. Thus far, Parliament was a unicameral institution in which the various social orders sat together. Although, in the early days, the knights of the shire (the county members) and the burgesses (the borough representatives) often went home once they had assented to new taxes, early English parliaments did not follow the continental model and sit as separate estates.

Then, in Edward III's reign, parliamentary developments destroyed any resemblance to other European assemblies, even if the concept of a society organised into estates lingered on in the minds of many men. Representatives of the lower clergy disappeared from Parliament and instead attended the Convocations (assemblies) of the Church. The knights and burgesses too began to sit apart from the bishops and abbots (the lords spiritual) and the nobles (lords temporal). However, the process of fragmentation stopped there. The lords spiritual and temporal did not divide into separate parliamentary estates. Instead, they, together with the King's professional counsel – his judges, attorney, solicitor and his serjeants (eminent lawyers) – continued to sit in the original Parliament House. It was not until well into the sixteenth century that they became known as the House of Lords. Nevertheless, long before Henry VII's reign Parliament had developed into a bicameral institution. Structurally, it bore little similarity to the continental concept of estates, even though it was common to refer to the lords spiritual and temporal and the commons as three estates.

This development was accompanied and followed by changes, not only in Parliament as an entity, but also in its component parts. Before the accession of the first Tudor in 1485 there had probably developed known procedures for the transaction of business, even if they were, as yet, flexibly applied. Surviving documentary fragments from the mid-fifteenth century show that clerks, in the Upper House at least, were keeping records of proceedings. The functions of parliaments, too, were altering and, at the same time, becoming more clearly defined. Consultation between the King and the wealthier, more powerful and influential subjects and communities in the realm continued to be crucial to good governance. And the parliament time was the most convenient occasion for the exchange of views. However, parliaments had shed their earlier curial (judicial) character. Despite continued references to 'the High Court of Parliament', they had become, first and foremost, taxing and legislative assemblies. Henry VII's parliaments did not simply declare what the law was, as a judge or law court might do; they enacted new laws on a wide range of subjects.

At the same time the Nether House of knights and burgesses had advanced in stature and authority. It alone could initiate the imposition of taxes on the laity. Furthermore, whereas the Commons had originally sought redress of grievances by petitions, which were then considered by the King, his legal counsel and great council, that too had altered. By the 1460s statute was enacted by the advice and assent of the bishops, abbots and peers, at the request of the Commons and 'by authority of Parliament'. In Henry VII's reign the Commons proceeded by bill – the first step towards an Act of Parliament – and its right to assent to new laws was recognised. So the Lower House (or House of Commons) had become constitutionally co-equal with the Upper. However, these were not early steps in some kind of rise to political supremacy. They were the simple consequences of a change whereby single-chamber parliaments became bicameral.

There was, in any case, considerable continuity with the medieval past. Parliaments remained royal occasions. They were summoned as and when the King wished, in order to furnish him with the necessary laws and supplementary revenue which would ensure good governance. He managed them in order to obtain what he wanted and he ended them as soon as they had performed their tasks to his satisfaction. Furthermore, the King remained outside and apart from parliaments. The correct way to describe the relationship is 'King and Parliament', a phrase which emphasises their separateness. Within parliaments, too, the changes should not be exaggerated. The Upper House, as the assembly of the social élite and the King's natural counsellors, enjoyed superior political status and wielded a formidable social influence. The presence of many of the nobles' kin, clients and servants in the Commons bolstered its authority in its dealings with a socially inferior house. Moreover, it inherited a much older parliamentary experience. By 1485 the Upper House had long enjoyed the bureaucratic services of a Chancery clerk, styled the Clerk of the Parliaments. It also benefited from the legal and legislative expertise of the King's professional counsel, who sat on woolsacks in the centre of the chamber, ready to advise and assist in the drafting of laws whenever they were called upon to do so.

Finally, it should be emphasised that the competence of parliaments (that is, the area of their legitimate activity) continued to be limited. Although the borderline was sometimes blurred, it was generally accepted that they could not encroach upon the spiritual authority of the Church or papacy, nor could they embark on a massive invasion of property rights. That had not altered by 1485. If there was change, then it was, in the short term, to the detriment of parliaments. The strong kingship of the pre-Tudor Yorkists, Edward IV and Richard III (1461–85), the Crown's restored financial solvency, and the Commons' grudging attitude to taxation reduced the royal necessity or desire for frequent assemblies. Nevertheless, their future was assured. Although parliaments were royal occasions, by 1485 they were also undoubtedly meetings of an institution. Parliament had its own procedures, clerical organisation, defined powers and corporate identity, and it was a recognised part of the machinery of government [43 *p. 144*].

2 PRE-REFORMATION PARLIAMENTS, 1485–1529

HENRY VII

The Lancastrian Henry VII continued the tradition of strong Yorkist kingship. His first, urgent priority was to secure the Tudor dynasty. This could be achieved only by political stabilisation, good governance, the elimination, neutralisation or recruitment of surviving Yorkists and the Crown's financial solvency. At first, parliaments were essential to the implementation of his policies and so they met frequently: in 1485, 1487, 1489, and 1491–92. Thereafter, as Henry's policies bore fruit, he needed them less. Only three met in the last eighteen years of his reign. None lasted more than eleven weeks and they averaged only eight to nine weeks apiece. There is nothing surprising in this. Parliaments were not a regular part of government. Short and infrequent sessions did not give rise to discontent. Quite the reverse. A Parliament usually meant a tax – never a popular prospect. The Commons was a niggardly provider. It hedged in its grants with often humiliating qualifications. In 1504 it stoutly resisted Henry's attempt to secure parliamentary approval for the levy of customary feudal aids. In any case, members of both houses could not have relished the prospect of winter travel, together with the costs and discomfort of London lodgings. Therefore Henry must have touched a responsive chord when he declared, in 1504, that 'for the ease of his subjects, without great, necessary, and urgent causes', he would not call another Parliament for a long time. By then his need of them had diminished. Few major laws were required. Furthermore, he preferred a thorough exploitation of hereditary revenues (together with an inexpensive, isolationist foreign policy), rather than parliamentary taxes, in order to achieve solvency and a reserve of treasure.

HENRY VIII

In 1509, however, Henry VII died and political circumstances changed dramatically. Henry VIII was the self-confident heir of his father's marriage-union of Lancaster and York. He was imbued with the ideals of chivalry and military prowess, inherited from the court of the Dukes of Burgundy, who had also ruled the Low Countries. His foreign policy was expansive, imperialistic and expensive. Military intervention in Europe cost money, and this simple fact meant a parliamentary resurgence. There were six sessions between 1510 and 1515. Furthermore, Henry relished cheap popularity. Therefore in 1510 he allowed Parliament (and especially the Commons) to voice governing-class discontent with his father's rigorous financial practices. Statutes, designed to prevent a recurrence, were enacted, whilst Richard Empson and Edmund Dudley, Henry VII's most conspicuous financial agents, were sacrificed.

Thomas Wolsey's rise to primacy under the King put an end to the brief parliamentary flurry of 1510–15. His autocratic distaste for parliaments was strengthened by Parliament's anti-clerical temper and especially by the Hunne case. Richard Hunne was a London merchant who refused to pay fees to the clergy for spiritual services. He was arrested on heresy charges and later found dead, in suspicious circumstances, in the Bishop of London's prison. The result was an anti-clerical outburst in the 1515 Parliament, during which the King, peers and Commons united against the isolated bishops and abbots in the Lords. Wolsey, who became Archbishop of York and cardinal, was concerned to protect clerical privilege. It is no wonder that only one more Parliament was summoned before his fall in 1529. When it met, in 1523, the government's request for war revenue received rough treatment from the Commons – an experience which confirmed his low opinion of parliaments.

Perhaps Henry too was disenchanted. Despite the life-grant of tunnage and poundage in 1510, frequent votes of fifteenths and tenths (a tax on moveables) and the innovation of a subsidy (income tax) in 1513, the actual yield was slow to come in and invariably considerably less than the estimated return. Exemptions and evasions, payment by instalments, administrative slowness, inefficiency and some dishonesty all played a part. In response to the request for a parliamentary tax in 1523 there was prolonged and heated debate in the Commons. It was not surprising. The Lower House, which alone initiated lay taxation at the King's request, was naturally sensitive about matters of the purse. Furthermore, the request was made as royal commissioners were still collecting a forced loan, which yielded the unprecedented sum of over £250,000 [39 *p. 119*]. Yet money was normally the primary purpose of parliaments, and after 1523 their future must have looked bleak. However, their extinction was not even a remote possibility. Political circumstances seldom remain static for long. Six years later a diplomatic humiliation and Wolsey's failure to secure the annulment of the King's first marriage led to the minister's fall. Henry, always the political realist and opportunist, turned back to Parliament.

INSTITUTIONAL DEVELOPMENTS

Far from being moribund, pre-Reformation parliaments showed signs of healthy institutional growth. The Clerk of the Parliaments gradually detached himself from Chancery, their traditional activating force and record repository. From 1497 he retained possession of the original Acts of Parliament, instead of transferring them to Chancery, and in 1515 he expanded the Lords' journal to include a daily attendance record. An embryonic Parliament Office emerged. At the same time the classic legislative process of three readings was taking shape. It evolved as the most practical contemporary way to make law. In the absence of printed copies of bills for members, the first reading was the literal recitation of the text of a proposed law. It was the only way to inform them of its contents. The second reading allowed debate on the bill's substance and an opportunity to propose amendments, which were usually incorporated by a committee. It was then engrossed (written on parchment). The third reading was concerned only with textual precision. As yet the process abounded with irregularities and imprecision. However, the movement towards the rigid procedural uniformity of Stuart parliaments was already under way in both houses, with the Lords probably taking the lead.

Known and consistent procedures were necessary because the early Tudor parliaments were such active legislative assemblies. Although their role as a point of contact and communication between Crown and governing class was important, their *raison d'être* was legislation. The King could secure new laws only with the assent of parliaments. Although the notion lingered on that they declared what the law was rather than made it, in practice early Tudor assemblies enacted an impressive volume of new laws. Many were public (concerning the whole country). They vested the Tudor dynasty with legality, strengthened royal government, voted taxes (which were cast in statutory form), imposed social controls and even tackled the delicate subject of benefit of clergy (which enabled not only those in holy orders but all who were literate to escape punishment by the King's courts for their first offence). There were legal reforms, confirmations of traitors' attainders and the restitution of their heirs, measures to protect landowners' property rights and manufacturers' markets, regulation of industrial standards and statutes penal (which punished offences, usually of an economic nature, with a fine or forfeiture). Other Acts were private. They were usually beneficial measures, affecting individuals, families, localities and particular economic interests. No corner of the realm and, with the possible exception of the general property rights of the governing class, no secular aspect of human affairs was exempt from the attentions of statute.

Parliaments were also becoming better equipped to transact legislative business. The Commons, which by the very nature of the political and social order had a less intimate connection with the King, needed guaranteed privileges in order to fulfil its responsibilities. The medieval Speaker had regularly requested personal access to the King, pardon if he misreported the sense of the House, and freedom from arrest for debts or other civil suits for Commons' members. The House strengthened its privileges during the pre-Reformation parliaments. Strode's case (1513) formally protected its members and its actions from the law courts. An Act of 1515 gave the House a measure of control over its members, when it empowered the Speaker to authorise their absence. Finally, in 1523, Sir Thomas More made the first known Speaker's request that members should be allowed to speak freely, without licence, on matters placed before them. These were not signs of the maturation or rise of the Commons, but a formalisation of basic privileges without which it could not function properly.

THE PARLIAMENTARY TRINITY

Last, but certainly not least, were the changing relations between King, Lords and Commons. These were the continuation of developments which ante-dated the Tudors. The Nether House finally achieved parity with the Upper. The judges' decision of 1489 made it clear that its assent was necessary to transform a bill into an Act. Another judicial ruling in 1516 effectively killed any lingering beliefs about Parliament as a gathering of estates. The judges declared that the bishops and abbots did not have to be present when a bill passed the Lords. In other words, they were simply members of one house in which decisions were taken by a majority vote, not a separate estate in a three-tiered assembly of estates. Finally, the King ceased to stand above and outside Parliament. By 1529, as the language of statutes attests, he had become an integral part of the institution. In a gradual, undramatic development, King and Parliament had been transmuted into one entity, the King-in-Parliament. If its competence remained limited, the critical decade of the 1530s was to demolish those limits and make it the sovereign authority in England and Wales.

3 THE PARLIAMENTS OF THE REFORMATION, 1529–58

THE PARLIAMENTS OF HENRY VIII

The catalyst of the dramatic change in the authority of parliaments during the 1530s was the so-called 'Divorce question' or, to be precise, the annulment of Henry VIII's first marriage. His motives were mixed: his infatuation (or love) for Anne Boleyn and the political necessity of discarding his ageing consort, Catherine of Aragon, in favour of a younger woman with child-bearing potential. In other words, the ruler's duty to sire an undisputed male heir and so guarantee a peaceful succession merged with the man's passion for a woman. The politics of 1529–36, during which the Reformation Parliament met seven times, were tortuous and complex and do not need to be unravelled here. It is enough to say that Henry secured his objectives through Parliament, which was the forum of an anti-clerical and largely anti-papal governing class. Between 1529 and 1532 it dutifully assisted him in his unsuccessful attempts to coerce Pope Clement VII, who alone could annul his marriage. Then, when Anne Boleyn's pregnancy in 1533 made a solution urgent, it passed the Act in Restraint of Appeals. This Act established its competence to deal in matters of spiritual law and enabled Henry to secure the annulment, marry Anne, and guarantee the legitimacy of their offspring. In 1533–34 Parliament proceeded to enact the statutory rejection of papal supremacy and the declaration of a national Catholic Church with the King as its supreme head.

The Reformation Parliament had served Henry well. It had resolved his matrimonial problems (for the time being). It had also effected a jurisdictional revolution in the Church and church-state relations, of which he was the chief beneficiary. However, Henry's resort to it was not a stroke of political genius. The Crown was powerless without the support of the governing class, which managed the realm under the King. The only convenient occasion on which he could consult it and harness its support was in Parliament. Nevertheless, Henry displayed an intuitive political skill during those years. He utilised the managerial and legislative talents of much abler men, such as Thomas Cromwell and Thomas Audley, and he retained the support of most members of the Lords and Commons with a judicious mixture of affability, tact and patience, criticism, threats and, occasionally, personal intervention. Naturally, opposition and criticism occurred in this crucial Parliament, but most of its major achievements were the consequence of a co-operative exercise between the government and the governing class.

Parliament also performed a vital role in the process of state-building during the 1530s. Whether the creation of a sovereign national state was a sudden, revolutionary event or simply the conclusion of a long evolutionary process, and whether it was the deliberate programme of Thomas Cromwell or a piecemeal response to Henry's matrimonial problems and the need to plug loopholes in national security and defences, these questions are still unresolved. Certainly, a case has been made for searching back before Cromwell's career for the intellectual origins of those changes [45; 49 *pp. 21–2*]. Whatever the answer to such questions, Parliament was central to the process of change. Statutes united England and Wales (1536 and 1543), suppressed franchises ('liberties' in which royal authority was severely limited) in 1536, dissolved the monasteries and transferred their property to the Crown (1536 and 1539–40), and equipped the state with laws to destroy its opponents. Parliamentary activity in the 1530s removed all customary limits on statute, which became the supreme and omnicompetent law – capable of dealing with anything. It altered or suppressed property rights on a massive scale when it dissolved monasteries, eliminated franchises and, in the statute of uses (1536), invalidated all bequests of land by will. Furthermore, although the King was simply recognised as the God-given head of the Church in 1534, later Henrician statutes elaborated and defined his power by authority of Parliament. Matters spiritual too had come within the competence of statute. Unlike *rex solus* (the King alone), whose power was limited and subject to the constraints of common law and statute, King-in-Parliament was now the sovereign authority in England [27; 29].

In the short term, this development strengthened the Crown. Parliaments repeatedly demonstrated their trust and devotion when they delegated legislative authority to Henry on such diverse matters as the incorporation of Wales (1536), religion (1540, 1543 and

1545), and the succession (1536 and 1544). In practice, Henry wielded a power unequalled by any other English monarch. Yet he also ensured the rapid decay of that power. The break with Rome and the infiltration of Protestantism into south-east England created a serious and growing religious division. Henry did not consistently support orthodox Catholicism, but, instead, subordinated religion to political expediency and left his young son's government in the hands of reformers. His wars against Scotland and France in the 1540s eroded the Crown's resources and made it more dependent on parliamentary revenue. In any case, there was no guarantee that, after his death, the Crown would continue to provide political leadership and the dynamic of change in Church and state.

PARLIAMENTS, 1547–58

Indeed, the troubled reigns of Edward VI (1547–53) and Mary I (1553–58) were marked by a decline in royal authority. It is true that Tudor government continued to direct the course of religious change: a Protestant reformation under Edward and a papal–Catholic restoration in Mary's reign. However, Protector Somerset's moderate Protestantism (1547–49), the Duke of Northumberland's more radical religious changes (1549–53) and the Marian reaction were all enacted by the explicit authority of Parliament. By 1558 there was no doubt that alterations in religion had to be embodied in statute. Moreover, inflation, economic recession, religious conflict, costly foreign wars, aristocratic misgovernment under Edward and unpopular Marian policies made mid-Tudor England a disturbed society. Inevitably there were parliamentary repercussions, often critical or hostile in nature: over the conduct of Edward's regency, Mary's Habsburg connection, religion, the fate of secularised property, and money. And the Crown's parliamentary leadership weakened as its financial dependence increased, at a time when its fortunes were entrusted first to noble governors and then to a woman and her Spanish consort.

INSTITUTIONAL DEVELOPMENTS

The sovereignty of the King-in-Parliament, together with the supremacy and omnicompetence of statute, were the most important institutional developments in the parliamentary history of this period. However, these were not the only changes. Parliaments were summoned more frequently, averaging one a year, and except for

Mary's troubled assemblies their sessions were longer. Their size and composition altered too. The Commons expanded from 296 to 400 members. This was the consequence of several developments. As one of the results of Cromwellian reorganisation, Wales was 'shired' and granted parliamentary representation [40; 100]. The need to find seats for Privy Councillors and other royal servants also led to the creation of parliamentary boroughs, especially on royal duchy lands. Other new seats resulted from private initiatives. Boroughs and local gentry, or their aristocratic patrons, persuaded the monarch to enfranchise a city, town or port. So the Commons inexorably grew and became ever more unwieldy. At the same time a fifteenth-century practice continued to grow as boroughs were invaded by non-resident carpet-bagging gentlemen, who were willing to serve without wages [54].

In contrast, the Upper House shrank dramatically. Until the 1530s the lords spiritual – bishops, abbots and priors – constituted a majority. The dissolution of the monasteries, however, removed the regular clergy. Despite Henry VIII's creation of six new bishoprics in 1540–42, the Lords was permanently secularised and its membership fell from more than one hundred to about eighty. Two-thirds of these were lords temporal (peers) who now sat by prescriptive right. The Lords' composition also changed rapidly. The processes of attrition (deaths from natural causes and state action) and recruitment were accelerated by the rapid twists of fortune during the Reformation. By 1558 over one-third of the peers summoned to Parliament had been ennobled in or after 1529. Bishops came and went with even greater rapidity as papists, Henrician Catholics, Edwardian Protestants and Marians rapidly succeeded each other. In one respect, however, Parliament experienced little change. Absenteeism remained a problem, especially in the Commons. The Lords' attendance improved, but this was due to particular circumstances: the disappearance of the abbots (whose record had been lamentable), the bishops' interest in religious changes, the nobles' participation in Edwardian government, and energetic parliamentary management by such ministers as Thomas Cromwell. Indeed, it was the Privy Council's prime managerial concern to secure, not the exclusion of opponents of royal policies, but the maximum presence which would ensure the transaction of royal business in parliaments [48].

The frequency with which the Crown enlisted the assistance of the two houses of Parliament, in order to effect so many great changes between 1529 and 1559, also accelerated another change. Members of the medieval House of Commons had been, above all, representatives of their communities. Their priorities, interests and grievances had been local. As the Tudors thrust upon them issues of political, religious and national importance, so they became more aware, concerned and active in the business of national government. In the process, Parliament was becoming something more than a point of contact: it was also a place where the interests of Crown and governing class could be balanced, and where that balance could be maintained and safeguarded [44].

During thirty years of hectic parliamentary activity, procedures and privileges continued to develop. Both houses advanced towards a uniform legislative procedure. More bills were referred to committees – indeed, in the 1530s a member described a bill which had been 'committed as the manner is'. Deviations from the three-reading norm gradually decreased from 46 per cent in the Lords in Henry VIII's first Parliament to 32 per cent in Mary's last. Privilege, however, focuses attention on the Commons. The Lords' members had a natural and continuous access to the monarch and, if the Bishop of Winchester was correct, there was 'free speech without danger' in the Upper House. The Commons too needed safeguards if it was to discharge its responsibilities effectively, especially when so much business was before it. Between Sir Thomas More's request for freedom of speech in 1523 and Mary's death in 1558, the Crown's grant of that privilege as an act of *grace* had become, to many members, a *right* formally acknowledged by the monarch. In 1550 the Commons also established the right to determine who was qualified to sit in the House. More important was the case of George Ferrers, a member who was arrested for debt in 1542. He was released, not by the Lord Chancellor's command as in the past, but by the order of the House. This action was not a challenge to the King's authority. Henry VIII intervened with a magisterial pronouncement in support of the Commons' privilege 'which he would not have to be infringed in any point'.

LEGISLATION AND POLITICS

The legislative record of the Reformation parliaments has already been touched on. It ranged over the entire spectrum of human affairs in Church and religion, state and commonweal. King-in-Parliament brooked no limits on its competence as it enacted far-reaching measures on Henry VIII's matrimonial arrangements, the succession, religious alterations and property rights. It transferred papal authority to the Crown (1533–34), funded the monarchy with ecclesiastical wealth (1536–40), settled religion on orthodox Catholic lines with the Act of Six Articles (1539), and inaugurated a Cromwellian programme of administrative, legal and social reform. Edwardian parliaments dismantled the punitive and deterrent machinery of Henrician statute, enacted a Protestant reformation and promulgated two prayer books (in 1549 and 1552). Mary's assemblies reversed most of the religious alterations since 1529, even if they would not restore secularised property to the Church. This bald summary ignores the many other officially inspired Acts on law and order, military reform, the social and economic problems which beset mid-Tudor England and, of course, the frequent grants of taxation.

Several important points must be borne in mind when considering the legislative record of the Reformation parliaments. Most important public measures were officially sponsored. Some of them did not pass without vocal criticism, heated debate and even obstinate resistance. Nevertheless, few foundered and were lost. The Crown continued to take the governing class into its confidence, seek its support, and achieve a high success rate. In any case, parliaments were reciprocal and benefited all interested parties. The novel competence of statute, and public confidence in Parliament as the answer to most problems, opened the flood-gates of legislation. Bills were submitted from localities, economic interests and individuals: towns and ports, both prospering and decaying; trading corporations; clothmakers and hatters, pewterers, bowyers and goldsmiths; reformers of the law, society and religion; courtiers, bishops and nobles. All were on hand with their written proposals. Although there was a Marian hiatus, when so much time was expended on the official programme in short sessions, the drift was unmistakable. Parliament, and especially the Commons which represented local communities, was inundated with local or personal legislation. At the same time the Lower House continued to grow in size and included a large number of parliamentary novices and uninterested members, anxious only to taste the fruits of the social season. The guidelines of Elizabethan parliamentary history were already being drawn: how to manoeuvre vital government bills through a large, ill-organised and over-burdened Commons.

Within this overall picture of parliamentary business, the legislative initiative and significance of the two houses fluctuated according to circumstances. The Lords started off with all the advantages. It was the older, more prestigious and organised House, whose members comprised the élites in Church and state. During the 1530s, however, two circumstances shifted the parliamentary centre of gravity to the Commons: Henry VIII's fear that opposition would centre on the bishops and abbots in the Lords; and the presence of his chief counsellor, Thomas Cromwell, in the Lower House. However, in 1539 the ennobled Cromwell took his seat in the Upper House and, in the following year, the remaining abbots disappeared. The legislative initiative swung back to the Lords and most official bills began there. Cromwell's fall in 1540 did not alter the situation. He had no successor as chief minister, and the most prominent Privy Councillors in Henry's last years were bishops and peers. In the following reign Edwardian noble Councillors dominated Parliament. Nevertheless, conservative resistance to the Edwardian religious reformation occurred in the Lords rather than in the Commons. Then, in Mary's early parliaments (1553–55), the Upper House abdicated its usual responsible parliamentary role. Instead, it sabotaged several of her most cherished measures and, in the process, sacrificed royal and public confidence. In contrast, criticism and resistance to royal measures were not frequently aroused in the Commons, and then only when the members detected a threat to their financial interests or property rights. Consequently, more government bills commenced in the Commons and the Lords' legislative role dramatically declined [47; 48; 53].

This change was due to the inter-connection between Court and Parliament. The conflict between Court factions (rival groupings of ambitious, aristocratic patrons and their client-followers) could have parliamentary consequences: the Aragonese faction supporting Henry VIII's first wife in the early 1530s; the neo-Lutheran Cromwell exploiting the religious conservatives in order to bring down Anne Boleyn (1536); the conservatives out-manoeuvring Cromwell on religion in 1539 and, a year later, securing his death by Act of attainder; Catherine Howard's death and the disgrace of her conservative Howard relatives (1542); and the Seymour–Herbert–Parr faction using statute to destroy the Howards in 1547. In Edward VI's reign regents, great nobles and aristocratic Councils managed the realm. They also fought amongst themselves and used parliaments to seal their victories over their rivals. As yet, however, the parliamentary effects of Court in-fighting were usually muted, and the victories of factions were concealed in the formal language of Acts of attainder. This changed in Mary's reign, when her Council was sharply divided. To some extent these divisions revealed differing attitudes to religion, the Pope's supremacy, Mary's marriage to a Spaniard, and Princess Elizabeth's place in the succession. More serious and divisive, however, were the perceived threats to secularised property, personality clashes and the struggle for influence between Stephen Gardiner, Bishop of Winchester, and William Lord Paget. Conciliar factions took their quarrels into the Lords, causing mayhem, aborting important royal bills and damaging the House's reputation as a responsible legislative body. Although it behaved with greater circumspection in the next Parliament (1555), the harm had been done and the Lords failed to restore public and royal confidence. That was the state of affairs when Elizabeth I became Queen in November 1558.

PART TWO: ANALYSIS

4 PARLIAMENT'S PLACE IN 1558–59

THE RIGHT PERSPECTIVE

It might be expected that, when Elizabeth's first Parliament assembled in January 1559, its members exuded an aggressive self-confidence. After all, during frequent meetings in the past thirty years, parliaments had destroyed all limits on the competence of statute. They had dealt with the highest matters of state, altered both religion and ecclesiastical organisation, encroached upon property rights in a drastic manner, and legislated on all aspects of the commonweal. In the process King(Queen)-in-Parliament had become sovereign. Many were slow to perceive the change, but by 1559 it had become generally accepted. A few years later Sir Thomas Smith could write in a matter-of-fact way that '[t]he most high and absolute power of the realm of England consisteth in the Parliament' [19 p. 78]. Furthermore, members of both houses had demonstrated their capacity and willingness to resist the government: over the annulment, schism and uses (a device which enabled landowners to avoid the payment of death duties to the Crown), the Edwardian reformation, aspects of the Marian programme and, sometimes, financial matters. At the same time the Crown's financial position had deteriorated, making it more dependent on parliamentary revenue.

Other developments were working against the Crown too. The prestige with which Henry VIII had invested the office had been eroded by the aristocratic regimes of Edward VI's reign and some unpopular features of Mary's Hispano-Catholic policies, the war with France in the interest of Spain and the demoralising loss of Calais in 1558. More serious in the long term were the inroads made by the Reformation on the natural loyalty to the monarch as God's anointed. By 1558 England had become a society deeply divided by the mutual hostility of Catholic and Protestant. Comprehension (the accommodation of most people within a broad national Church) or toleration had no chance of success in 1558. The new monarch would have to be a partisan ruler, with her feet firmly planted in either the Protestant or Catholic camp – especially if, after the Marian interlude, Church and state were once again united under the Crown. According to their religious predilections, subjects would have to decide whether to obey their 'godly' prince or resist their 'ungodly' prince. There were already ominous precedents for the future. In the previous reign exiled Protestants had published attacks on Queen Mary and justifications of resistance, deposition and even tyrannicide. Elizabeth would rule a society in which allegiance and obedience to her as Queen and God's lieutenant were no longer automatic and unquestioning. Moreover, she was young, inexperienced and, after the painful experience of Mary, yet another woman in a male-dominated political system. Therefore it might be reasonable to assume that, when the Lords and Commons assembled in January 1559, they would dictate the terms of the New Order.

In fact, this was not so. The monarch still determined when a Parliament met and how long it should last. Despite the frequency and the critical nature of parliaments in the past thirty years, they had not acquired the capacity to coerce the Crown into particular courses of action. Both houses could be obstructive, but they did not make grants of taxation dependent on the redress of grievances ('redress before supply'). Nor did they try to impose governing-class policies on the Crown. It was recognised that policy-making was the monarch's prerogative and, if nobles, bishops and gentlemen attempted to alter royal policies, they did so by lobbying through the Court and Council. They did not use parliaments, which were not a continuous part of royal government but an irregular supplement, providing the extra money and new laws which it required [*Doc. 1*]. Furthermore, parliaments remained, in 1558 as in 1529, an essential line of communication between the Crown and governing class – what G.R. Elton termed a 'point of contact' [23]. This was a two-way process of consultation, advice and information on matters both of high policy and local concern. The occasion of Parliament also enabled ambitious careerists to seek out patrons, catch the monarch's attention and, by a loyal and able performance, launch themselves on a career in royal service. However, parliamentary expectations were not confined to such men. Each meeting provided valuable opportunities for all members of the governing class to obtain beneficial legislation for themselves and needful laws for the commonweal. In these various ways parliaments were important expressions of the consensus politics which the Tudor establishment cherished. The Reformation crisis and its often abrasive politics had not destroyed or diminished these parliamentary priorities.

In any case, the important on-going relationship between the Crown and governing class lay not in Parliament but in the localities, where nobles and gentlemen administered at the royal command. Doubtless many of them in 1558 had their own ideas about the future direction of religion, the most important reason for calling Elizabeth's first Parliament. And they would act as a mirror of the political nation's needs, concerns and fears. Nevertheless, they came in answer to Elizabeth's summons, and they would wait patiently until she indicated her intentions. The parliamentary initiative remained with the monarch.

THE HISTORIOGRAPHY OF ELIZABETHAN PARLIAMENTS

Three different explanations of the significance of Elizabethan parliaments have held the stage during this century. The earliest of these rested on the belief that, over the centuries, parliaments evolved upwards, from an assembly which was strictly subordinate to the Crown to the supreme constitutional authority and seat of representative government. Within this long-term evolutionary development, however, was an aberration, during which parliaments were obedient, even subservient, to a Tudor despotism.

This interpretation gradually gave way before a new one, which was just as evolutionary but with a vital difference. The Tudor parliaments were cast in a new role. They were not acquiescent but increasingly assertive, and they provided an essential continuity between the rising medieval and Stuart assemblies. Indeed, Tudor parliaments bequeathed an apprenticeship in the arts of opposition which their early Stuart successors inherited and developed.

The chief architects and proponents of this second interpretation were A.F. Pollard [35], J.E. Neale [71; 72], and W. Notestein [73]. They propounded the rise of Tudor parliaments and, within them, a shift of authority from a declining House of Lords to a 'maturing' and more self-confident House of Commons. Furthermore, they argued, conflict and opposition to royal policies steadily grew during the century until, in Elizabeth's reign, there emerged, in the Lower House, a novel kind of opposition. It was persistent, organised and not, as in the past, merely obstructive. It came armed with its own programme, an alternative to Elizabethan policies. Neale demonstrated this with his discovery of the 'puritan choir', which was busy in the parliaments of 1563–66/67 and 1571, and his study of the concerted Presbyterian agitations in the 1580s. Although the Commons' attack on the Queen's grant of harmful monopolies in 1597 and 1601 was not the work of an organised opposition (see pp. 54–5), he showed how its spontaneous anger could force her into surrender. By the end of the reign it had become a power to be reckoned with. Neale's thesis gained further credence from the work of Notestein, whose particular interest was early Stuart parliamentary history. Notestein charted the process, beginning under Elizabeth, by which the Crown's control of the Commons through the Speaker, a royal nominee, and the Privy Council was undermined by a parliamentary opposition (see pp. 40–3, 53–4). Building on these late Elizabethan foundations, a recalcitrant Lower House seized the parliamentary initiative from the Crown in the early seventeenth century.

This version of Tudor parliamentary history became so widely accepted in the mid-twentieth century that it is sometimes referred to as the orthodox interpretation. It rested on a number of priorities, above all an awareness of the civil war to come and a consequent search for links between the Elizabethan parliamentary experience and that cataclysmic event. Neale was open and honest when he wrote that 'my purpose is to reveal the significance of the Elizabethan period in the constitutional evolution of England, and, more specifically, to banish the old illusion that early-Stuart Parliaments had few roots in the sixteenth century' [72, I *p. 11*]. Secondly, indeed because of this purpose, Parliament was studied as a political institution whose prime function was to criticise, limit and challenge royal authority. Its records, procedures, privileges and management by the Council were examined to provide evidence of this function. There was a search for examples of conflict and confrontation, resulting in a selective and episodic concentration on matters of heat and 'great moment'. In particular, attention focused on the cradle of political liberties, the Commons, which was flexing its political muscle in Elizabeth's reign. In contrast, the House of Lords was neglected or dismissed, because it was assumed to be in decline and little more than a subservient tool of the Crown: as Neale commented, 'It is well to remember that the function of a Tudor House of Lords was less to impede the Crown than to assist it in controlling the Commons' [72, I *p. 41*]. Finally, Neale inherited and adopted Pollard's biographical interest. But whereas Pollard wrote about great men – Henry VIII, Wolsey and

Protector Somerset – Neale applied biographical techniques to lesser men on a large scale. He and his students amassed a great quantity of biographical information about the knights and burgesses of the Commons. This enabled him to chart the continuing invasion of borough seats by non-resident gentlemen (in itself a breach of the law) and to identify the twin dynamics of an assertive Lower House as an educated gentry and Puritanism. This was consistent with his intention to explain why the Commons rose – the first steps on the road to civil war.

Few questioned this orthodoxy until the 1970s and early 1980s, when there emerged not a different school but a different approach. The pioneer and pre-eminent advocate of this fresh way of looking at parliaments was G.R. Elton [23; 24; 26; 27; 29; 65; 66]. In 1971 he lamented historians' almost habitual treatment of the institution 'as a political arena in which political conflicts were fought out and major political changes carried through' [25 *p. 7*]. Parliament's chief function and purpose was not political debate but the making of law – although, of course, the latter might generate the former. Elton asked what historians might learn if they altered their priorities and concentrated on the development of law-making procedures and the legislative output. The enactment of statute necessitated the assent of monarch, Lords, and Commons, and so new or amended laws were the end products of a co-operative exercise between them [25].

During the next two decades, Elton and a number of other historians pursued this line of enquiry. It was institutionally, not politically, oriented, and therefore it asked different questions. What were the functions of parliaments? How did they carry them out? What were the expectations of all parties to the parliamentary process? New questions provided a fresh way of looking at things and provided some surprising revelations. Most parliamentary time was devoted to law-making and much of it to legislation of a personal or parochial kind, not to great issues and the needs of the Crown [93; 95; 112–18; 120–1; 127]. Procedures and privileges were refined in order to facilitate the transaction of humdrum legislative business, rather than to strengthen the Commons in its confrontations with the monarch. Conciliar management was necessary to ensure that parliaments were co-operative and therefore successful and productive for both the government and the governing class. It was not a controlling mechanism, to be challenged and overthrown by a parliamentary opposition centred in the Commons [132–6].

The House of Lords too received the attention of the 'revisionist' historians. It could no longer be relegated to the inferior place assigned to it in the orthodox interpretation. Parliament was a trinity and the assent of all three members was necessary to make, amend or repeal a law [*Doc. 2*]. Furthermore, the Tudor Lords had already demonstrated its political muscle before Elizabeth's reign. Its religious conservatism had been a cause of concern to Henry VIII's government in the 1530s and an obstacle to the statutory enactment and enforcement of the Edwardian Protestant Reformation. In the Marian parliaments of 1553–55, powerful faction leaders, operating through the Upper House, frustrated or delayed important official measures, such as those to punish heretics, exiles and traitors [46–8]. Although royal confidence in its loyalty and responsibility was shaken, at least its conduct illustrates that it was not a political cypher. This was demonstrated yet again when conservative resistance to the Elizabethan Settlement of 1559 was centred there (see pp. 25–7).

Apart from the temporary Marian aberration, and despite its capacity for conservative resistance during the Reformation, the Tudor House of Lords was the more efficient and effective legislative chamber. Fewer bills were initiated there than in the Commons, but a higher proportion of them passed into law. To some extent it was simply the beneficiary of its age: as the older house its procedures and records were at a more advanced stage of development. As a chamber of life-members its collective experience far outstripped that of the Commons. It was served by the matchless legal advice and bill-drafting skills of the Queen's judges and a common law élite of serjeants-at-law. Furthermore, its membership was the noble and episcopal élite of the English state, Church and society. Historians engaged in parliamentary revision have been particularly conscious of this last point, because they have endeavoured to set the institution in the context of the Elizabethan social structure. This has revealed the many inter-cameral links between noble patrons in the Lords and their relations and clients in the Commons – a social influence which must be added to the formal authority of the Upper House, if its parliamentary role is to be correctly assessed (see pp. 33–4).

To some extent because of its critical response to the Whig interpretation, but chiefly by the very nature, priorities and parameters of its concerns, revisionism has been perceived by some to minimise, ignore, and even implicitly deny the co-existence of important and contentious issues. The promotion of local bills by economic interests, especially but not only those of London; the refinement of management techniques and the importance of parliamentary managers, especially those entrusted with the Crown's parliamentary objectives; the development of an archive and a clerical organisation, which emphasised that Parliament was a permanent institution, not merely a series of events: none of these particular revisionist concerns bore any relationship, for example, to Neale's Elizabethan picture of parliaments characterised by conflict and opposition. Indeed, as revisionism dealt with petty and local matters, techniques designed to facilitate productivity and developments to improve institutional efficiency, it was, by its very nature, a stark contrast to the whiggish focus on high politics, controversy, resistance to the Crown and the Commons' apprenticeship to power.

In 1986 G.R. Elton's *The Parliament of England, 1559–1581* [66] provided the first thorough published study of legislation, which revisionists rightly regarded as the chief purpose and function of parliaments. It combined a detailed research piece with a synthesis of revisionists' published work. And in this study Elton kept faith with the belief which he had stated in 'The Body of the Whole Realm' in 1969: that whilst Tudor parliaments 'were, as they always had been, arenas for debate, argument, opposition, resistance to royal claims, the working out of compromises', their true functions were to assist government with supply and legislation 'as the ultimate embodiment of the nation in political action' [24 *p. 59, 61*]. Whilst, in *The Parliament of England,* Elton acknowledged that sessions were not devoid of disputes, heated debate, or outright opposition, he insisted that these were not characteristic but rather episodes in otherwise productive parliaments.

None of this conclusively proves that the revisionist historians are on the right lines or that the orthodox school has got it all wrong. Undoubtedly, revisionism has convincingly demolished some aspects of the older political interpretation, thrown others into doubt, and disproved a number of its most important conclusions. Moreover, proceeding as it does from institutional, not political, priorities, it has advanced our knowledge of parliaments – what they did, how they worked and what was expected of them. In the process, however, it has identified new areas in which ignorance reigns and research urgently needs to be done. More serious, perhaps, is the danger of a distorted picture produced by the institutional approach of the revisionists and their rejection of the political interpretation. In the later 1980s criticism was voiced that in their concentration on productivity, business and collaboration, revisionists were indeed tending to belittle or ignore serious parliamentary disagreement or conflict. Instead, they were focusing attention on the petty politics of parochial and economic interests, which sought to promote their own bills or obstruct others (see pp. 72–5). In the Neale Memorial Lecture in 1987 Professor Patrick Collinson expressed such a concern. He cited the case of a member of the Elizabethan Commons, James Morrice, who landed in hot water for criticising the Archbishop of Canterbury, despite the Queen's ban on discussion of Church affairs. Morrice complained that bills on petty matters such as 'the shipping of fish' could be discussed freely, but not 'the great things of the law and public justice'. Collinson echoed Morrice's complaint: 'I hope that it is not yet the case that historians of these Parliaments are to be subject to the same sort of inhibitions as those assemblies themselves, forbidden to mention great things but only permitted to speak of the shipping of fish' [131 *p. 207*]. Such criticism was both significant and, to some extent, justified. It was also acknowledged by some revisionists, such as David Dean who, in 1989, wrote, 'It is now time . . . to put the politics back into parliament and to put parliaments back into the political history of the period' [22 *p. 411*].

THE ELIZABETHAN SETTLEMENT, 1559

Although ardent Protestants hailed Elizabeth as their deliverer, her prospects of success were remote in November 1558. She became Queen of a demoralised, deeply divided, militarily weak and economically enfeebled realm. Domestic problems – disrupted trade, inflation, a debased coinage, the state's indebtedness, plague and religious conflict – were enough to occupy the wholehearted attention of the Queen, but that was not all. Her diplomatic position was perilous. She inherited a Spanish military alliance and a joint war against Scotland and France, the only 'bitter' fruit of which had been the loss of Calais. Although peace negotiations were under way, any precipitate move to Protestantism (if she intended to move in that direction) would probably alienate her negotiating partner, Catholic Spain. This would complete her diplomatic isolation. Rome had declared that Elizabeth was a bastard and acknowledged Mary Stuart, consort of the French King and herself Queen of Scotland, as the legitimate successor of Mary Tudor. Meanwhile, a French army sat in Scotland with no effective English force capable of preventing its southward march to London if it chose.

It was a hazardous time and required a circumspect ruler. Yet a settlement of religion was urgent and would brook no delay. Furthermore, as the Marian restoration of Catholicism and papal supremacy had been effected by statute, any alteration of religion or Church–state relations would require parliamentary sanction. Perhaps Elizabeth contemplated the options open to her: the Roman Catholicism of her half-sister, the national Catholicism of her father, or some form of Protestantism. If she did, there is little doubt that she quickly discarded the first of these. Marian Catholicism was identified with foreign, Spanish rule and the burning of English heretics. Henrician Catholicism, which combined royal supremacy with traditional religion, was perhaps more acceptable to Elizabeth. The problem is that her religious opinions were, to a large extent, concealed by a mixture of ambiguity and silence. Some of her conservative personal preferences were clear enough: Catholic vestments, ornaments and ritual, the office of bishop and celibacy of clergy. Such conservatism must have influenced her choice of options. Political realities and national preferences, however, could also affect her thinking: on the one hand, an active Protestant reforming impulse amongst some of her subjects; on the other, the existence of so many who were conservative or undecided. Nevertheless, her personal theological position remains an enigmatic one. Any interpretation of the Elizabethan Settlement must be conditional on this fact, especially as so little is known about the legislative process which produced the Acts of supremacy and uniformity [34 *pp. 97– 101*; 63 *p. 77*; 70 *p. 135*].

In any case Elizabeth had to tread warily, because of the delicate diplomatic situation. Lord Keeper Bacon's opening address to the two houses on 25 January 1559 was couched in general terms and gave no more than a hint of her intentions and wishes [*Doc. 3*]. Moreover, the official bill to restore the royal supremacy over the Church was not introduced until 9 February. The process whereby this bill, together with a measure on religious uniformity, became law was tortuous, lengthy and complex, and it has been explained in a number of ways. Prominent Elizabethans such as John Foxe and William Camden portrayed the Protestant heroine Elizabeth, loyally supported by a Protestant House of Commons, overcoming the resistance of Catholic prelates and peers in the Lords in order to create a national Protestant Church governed by Queen and bishops. If this was a piece of propaganda, it was certainly effective, because it was accepted and repeated for nearly 400 years. Then J.E. Neale, in a brilliant and imaginative exercise, demolished the traditional interpretation [72, I *pp. 42–84*]. The Elizabethan Settlement, in his view, was the product of a tussle between a conservative Queen and members of her faithful but radical Puritan Commons, who sought a more Calvinistic Church. In the end she conceded more than she would have preferred. Neale's thesis, persuasively argued, turned the old interpretation on its head. In the process it transferred the parliamentary dynamic from the Lords to the Commons. This had the merit of consistency, because it fitted neatly into his picture of a rising, assertive Lower House and a declining Upper Chamber.

Neale's interpretation won general acceptance until the advent of Norman Jones [101]. He re-examined the old sources, utilised more recently available evidence, and concluded that, whilst both of the previous explanations were guilty of over-simplification, the older one corresponded more closely to the facts. Neale assumed, rather than proved, the existence of a disciplined and active body of Puritan knights and burgesses in the Commons. Supposedly, they were led by Marian exiles who had returned from Frankfurt, Strasburg and Geneva – the centres of reformed religion. And they worked together, with some success, to bend the Queen to their will. However, not all of those members who had gone abroad in Mary's reign had been 'religious' exiles. Nor did those who had done so act as a cohesive Protestant pressure group in the Commons in 1559. Indeed, some had close ties with the government. As a consequence, Neale's Puritan 'campaign' evaporated. Jones concluded that the most serious problems facing Elizabeth were the dangers inherent in the diplomatic situation and the obstinate resistance of Catholics in the Lords. Certainly the facts support him. Viscount Montagu, Archbishop Heath, Bishop Scot (Chester) and Abbot Feckenham (Westminster) spoke at length and delivered wide-ranging attacks on the proposed religious settlement [*Docs 4, 5, 6*]. In a Lords' committee, opponents of the first supremacy bill secured its drastic alteration [101 *pp. 99–101*] and, in a valiant rearguard action, they voted against each step in the enactment of the new religious order. Doubtless they drew encouragement from the firm Catholic support of the Convocation of Canterbury. On the other hand, the inconclusive public disputation between Catholics and Protestants (31 March and 3 April) gave Elizabeth an opportunity to weaken the conservatives when she imprisoned their most obdurate spokesmen, John White (Winchester) and Thomas Watson (Lincoln).

By the time Parliament was dissolved on 8 May 1559 a new

national Church had been established. If Elizabeth was only supreme governor (a lay supervisor) by authority of Parliament and not, like Henry VIII, supreme head (with spiritual authority) appointed by God [*Docs 7, 8*], the difference would matter little in practice. Insofar as the rest of the Elizabethan Settlement is a reflection of her wishes, it is not evidence of her firm Protestantism. She retained the Catholic office of bishop and the traditional hierarchy of Church courts. And, although the order of worship was based on the more radical prayer book of 1552, nevertheless it incorporated a modified definition of the sacrament of the altar, together with traditional vestments and ritual. Insofar as Elizabeth had scored an impressive parliamentary success over entrenched Catholicism in the Lords, the initial and central issue had been Church government. The Queen and the Marian bishops might have found common ground in the maintenance of Catholicism, if this fundamental and insoluble difference had not divided them.

Members of the Upper House had demonstrated their independent temper and their willingness to resist the monarch and the Privy Council, just as they had done in 1553–55. On the other hand, the parliamentary role of the Crown now changed. For thirty years, since 1529, it had provided the leadership and dynamic for alterations in religion. Whatever Elizabeth's position was at the time of her first Parliament, thereafter she became the arch-conservative and the defender of the *status quo*. So the initiative for change passed to her Privy Council and her governing class.

5 MEMBERSHIP AND ATTENDANCE

THE LORDS' MEMBERSHIP

Not only the composition but also the physical structure of the Elizabethan House of Lords [*Doc. 9*] were strong reminders of the way in which parliaments had originated and developed as meetings of the monarch, his professional counsel and his great council (see p. 1). So too were the designated names of its venue – the Parliament House – and its chief bureaucrat, the Clerk of the Parliaments. Only the Queen (who did not attend business sessions), the lords spiritual and temporal, the legal assistants and the clerks might proceed beyond the 'bar' or rail running across the lower end of the chamber. In contrast, the Commons' members, who crowded in behind their Speaker to attend the opening and closing ceremonies of Parliament, could not. This symbolised the fact that the knights and burgesses had begun as an afforcement, not an integral part, of parliaments.

Neither the size nor the composition of the Upper House underwent any dramatic changes after Elizabeth's first Parliament. The number of bishoprics remained constant at twenty-six throughout the reign, whilst the peerage fluctuated between fifty-five and sixty-two. However, changes did occur and they were more significant than these figures suggest. This was because of Elizabeth's conduct in the matter of peerage creations and episcopal appointments. She was parsimonious to a fault in the grant of honours, creating only two earls (Leicester and Nottingham), one viscount (Bindon) and seven barons. Eight other titles were revived, restored, or inherited by marriage or descent through a woman. This was a lean harvest in a long reign of forty-five years and it was more than balanced by natural wastage and six attainders for treason. Consequently, the number of peers at her accession – fifty-seven – had actually fallen to fifty-five by 1603. Even so, by then the combined effects of loss and gain had substantially altered the composition of the peerage, one-third of which owed its noble rank to the Queen. The process of change, however, was a long and gradual one. In contrast, the episcopate experienced a violent, traumatic spasm when Elizabeth, as supreme governor, purged it after the enactment of the religious settlement in 1559. All but one of the bishops – Kitchin of Llandaff – refused to accept the new religious order and were replaced. Furthermore, the Abbot of Westminster and the Prior of St John of Jerusalem, who were the only parliamentary fruits of Mary's monastic revival, were removed when their religious orders were once again dissolved.

Elizabethan peers were eligible to attend parliaments, except for those disabled by the usual conditions of minority, poverty and the priorities of royal service. In addition, there were political prisoners, in particular the Earl of Hertford who, during the 1560s, committed the double offence of marrying Lady Catherine Grey, a claimant to succeed Elizabeth, without royal permission and then of siring a child whilst they were in the Tower. In 1572 the Duke of Norfolk (executed for treason during the session), the Earls of Arundel and Southampton, and Lords Cobham and Lumley were implicated in varying degrees in the anti-Cecil, pro-Catholic conspiracies of 1569–72. Furthermore, in 1601, shortly after the execution of the Earl of Essex, his ally, Southampton, was imprisoned for life and the Queen commanded five of his supporters – Bedford, Rutland, Montagu, Cromwell and Sandys – to absent themselves from her last Parliament. The bishops, it is true, were now less likely to fall victims to royal displeasure as a result of sudden religious changes. On the other hand, the supreme governor was notoriously lax in her ecclesiastical management. She left sees vacant for many years in order to pocket the revenues or provide pensions for courtiers: Bristol for a decade, Ely for eighteen years and Oxford for forty-one. The net result was that the episcopate, which numbered no more than one-third of the House when it was at full strength, was always undermanned when parliaments met.

Therefore the Lords was exclusive, select, and above all few in number. It averaged eighty to ninety on paper and always less in practice. Certainly it was rich in experience, not only of government but also of Parliament. Unlike knights and burgesses in the Commons, Elizabethan bishops and peers continued to be life-tenants of their seats, subject only to the hazards of Tudor politics and religious change. Moreover, some new peers, who had sat in the Commons, carried up with them a knowledge of its procedures and politics [132 *p. 218*]. Nevertheless, when they entered the Lords they became members of a small chamber which was diminishing in size.

THE COMMONS' MEMBERSHIP

The Commons' growth was both a vivid contrast to the Lords and a paradox. Until Edward VI's reign its members jammed into the chapter house of Westminster Abbey, close to the Palace in which the bishops and peers deliberated. Then it was assigned the equally cramped chapel of St Stephen, within the precincts of Westminster Palace itself. Whether or not this belatedly symbolised its advancement to equal status with the Lords, which was already housed there, it was not a significant improvement in its accommodation. Certainly it must have been an uncomfortable experience for the 400 members who were elected in 1559. Moreover, the Commons had only one committee room, no place to store its records, and suffered from the continuous nuisance caused by the presence of members' servants and pages on the stairs leading to the chamber [71 *pp. 364–7*].

Herein lies the paradox – inferior accommodation for a much larger assembly – and also the vivid contrast: the fact that, unlike the shrinking Upper House, its membership continued to grow – from 400 to 462. As enfranchisement was the Crown's right, it is reasonable to speculate whether this process was an attempt to return more royal nominees, or at least loyalists. After all, sixteen new members were returned for boroughs in Cornwall and Lancashire, where royal duchies had extensive landholdings and social influence, and six in the Isle of Wight, of which Elizabeth's kinsman, Sir George Carey, was captain. In this respect there was continuity between her reign and those of her Tudor predecessors. It was important, for managerial purposes, to ensure the election of Privy Councillors and prominent royal servants. Borough enfranchisements were often designed to serve that end [54]. On the other hand, many new constituencies were the result of the workings of the patronage system. Powerful courtier-patrons secured representation for their clients, both corporate and individual. So Carey persuaded the Queen to enfranchise Newport, Newtown and Yarmouth in the Isle of Wight. Thereafter he was able to influence their elections and even nominate some of their members. Pressure to enlarge the Commons derived, not only from the centre, but also from patrons anxious to gratify clients.

Although Elizabeth created thirty-one parliamentary boroughs, each returning two members, she did not reinforce county representation. Each English shire continued to elect two knights and each Welsh county one. Yet the country gentry were becoming more numerous and more of them were interested in serving a term in the Commons, as a token of their status or as part of their political apprenticeship. Frustrated by the lack of available shire seats, which were increasingly the preserve of the most important county families, lesser gentlemen had to turn elsewhere. This pressure both caused the growth in the number of seats and accelerated the invasion of boroughs by carpet-bagging (non-resident) gentry. Even then, however, they often had to compete with lawyers, local burgesses and merchants from the big cities, especially London. Elizabeth might well protest in 1579 'that there are over-many [burgesses] already' [11, I *p. 117*], but the tide of importunate suitors was hard to stem. Indeed, so strong was the pressure that the fifteenth-century statutes requiring elected knights and burgesses to be residents were consistently ignored. According to the law, burgesses should have comprised 75–80 per cent of the House and country gentlemen the rest. In practice, however, the proportions were reversed. It is a pleasant irony that many of the nation's law-makers were only able to sit in the Commons by a collective and continuous collusive action to defeat the law. Conscience, and perhaps a sense of guilt, occasionally surfaced, as in 1571, when members debated a bill designed to end the residential qualification of members [*Doc. 10*]. However, the legislators left matters as they were and went on their illegal way, regardless of the Queen's strictures on the subject [*Docs 11, 15*].

In some respects the seating arrangements in St Stephen's chapel emulated those of the Parliament House: the Speaker occupied a raised seat at the upper end of the chamber; below him the Underclerk of the Parliaments sat at a table; and at the lower end was a rail behind which offenders, suitors and their legal counsel might plead. There the similarities ended. In the Upper House the bishops and nobles occupied benches placed on the floor, but, as John Hooker, one of Exeter's members in 1571, explained, the Commons' chamber was 'framed and made like unto a theatre, being four rows of seats one above another, round about the house' and even around the Speaker's chair. And whereas the lords spiritual and temporal sat in strict order of rank and precedence, each knight and burgess 'sitteth as he cometh, no difference being there held of any degree, because each man in that place is of like calling' [71 *pp. 364–5*]. However, there were significant exceptions: the Queen's

Privy Councillors sat on the lowest row about the Speaker, where they could advise and prompt him, and next to them on the right sat the members of England's two largest cities, London and York. The crucial nature of this juxtaposition will be considered later (see pp. 72–3). However, the House did not regard the arrangement as a politically sinister attempt to manipulate it. Indeed, it was accepted as right and natural, and a member who tried to breach the time-honoured practice received a firm repulse [*Doc. 12*].

THE IMPORTANCE OF THE PATRON–CLIENT RELATIONSHIP

Elizabethan parliaments were a microcosm of a homogeneous governing class, and their membership naturally reflected its characteristic bonds, such as common political priorities, life-style and devotion to the Crown, kinship, and the patron–client relationship. The last of these was vital to political stability, even though it could have a divisive effect. Although, on their own initiative and without advice, Tudor monarchs advanced a favoured few to high office, title and fortune, grants of patronage were usually royal responses to recommendations. These could succeed only if a man had access to the Queen and if he was of such standing and trust that his recommendation was likely to be granted. Such a man – courtier, noble, royal servant – became a patron to whom lesser mortals – clients – flocked in the hope of securing advancement. A patron sought benefits for his clients. They, in return, gave him material rewards, out of gratitude, and enlarged his public presence (following), out of loyalty, thereby impressing the Tudor political world with his greatness.

Whilst great men had patronage of their own to distribute, the increased income and presence of a patron depended, above all, on his ability to extract favours from the Queen. However, men's expectations were much greater than the Crown's capacity to fulfil them. The Elizabethan state was poor and growing poorer as inflation, land sales and the costs of war reduced its capital and income. At the same time the governing class – the group seeking royal largess – was growing in size. Human cupidity, together with the Crown's poverty, intensified competition for a share of a smaller patronage-cake, with the result that patrons and clients formed into pressure-groups or factions for that purpose. Factions were active both in the localities – the political world of most men – and at Court, where alone careers and fortunes could be made. And sometimes they also advocated specific policies – the belligerent Leicester favouring war and the economy-conscious Burghley preferring peace. No matter whether factions sought policy decisions or patronage, the Queen had to be persuaded [*99 pp. 1–12*].

However, not only Elizabeth but all patrons were under pressure to provide benefits, one of which was election to the Commons. This was not a sign of the growing authority and importance of the Lower House. For a variety of reasons – social, economic, occupational, local and personal – more gentlemen, lawyers and merchants wanted to sit in Parliament. The House of Lords was closed to them, whilst great gentlemen or peers' sons monopolised shire seats in the Commons. There was only one alternative, the parliamentary boroughs. Aristocratic patrons (and some bishops too) entered into electoral politics, using their influence as landowners, courtiers, employers, royal servants or protectors of borough interests to place their clients [132]. They were frequently successful, because Tudor elections were concerned with representing organic communities, not bodies of electors who exercised a modern democratic right of adult suffrage. What mattered was how well a borough's interests were promoted by its representatives, not how they were elected. So the Privy Council could intervene with impunity at Gatton (where the Catholic Copley family owned the borough and normally chose the members) in order to ensure the return of suitable burgesses [*Doc. 13*]. Borough suffrage ranged from all the burgesses, as at Bedford, to the deserted Old Sarum (controlled by the Earls of Pembroke) and the Packington family's personal choice in Aylesbury. Such proprietary boroughs (owned by an individual or family) and small, decayed or poor townships were tempting targets for 'borough-hunting' patrons. Aristocratic intervention in parliamentary elections may seem strange, alien, and certainly undemocratic, but it was often of mutual advantage. Patrons could satisfy clients and, at the same time, offer candidates who would serve boroughs well without demanding the statutory wage of two shillings a day – a burdensome amount for small communities [*Doc. 14*]. In any case, some, especially the wealthier and more independent cities and towns, rejected such aristocratic pressures [*Doc. 14*].

This kind of electoral activity was not new, but it was growing and it affected both the Commons' composition and the links between members of the two houses. Forty per cent of the sixty to seventy-five borough members elected for Cornwall, Devon and Dorset between 1559 and 1584 'can certainly be associated with [the second Earl of] Bedford and their returns attributed to him, alone or in conjunction with Sir William Cecil, Lord Burghley' [79, I *pp.* 60–2]. It should be added, however, that Bedford's electoral influence was in decline before his death in 1585. Furthermore, some clients did not depend on their aristocratic patrons in order to secure election to the Commons. A systematic survey indicates that the 'influence of a great man' played some part in the election of about one-third of borough members [79, I *p. 59*]. However, such figures need to be used with caution because the evidence of influence is often insubstantial or illusory [118 *pp.* 76–7]. In the same way almost seventy office-holders in the Exchequer were elected to the Elizabethan Commons. They were not, as has sometimes been assumed, a parliamentary interest under the active leadership of the Lord Treasurer in the Upper House. Their election and activity were more often than not the consequences of personal influence and choice [130]. Nonetheless, the existence of parliamentary clienteles of prominent nobles, such as the Earls of Bedford and Leicester, illustrates the homogeneity of the governing class as it was mirrored in parliaments and the way in which the network of relationships cut across the formal bicameral division into Lords and Commons [129].

ATTENDANCE AND THE PROBLEM OF ABSENTEEISM

It would be wrong to assume that, when Parliament was summoned, there was a frantic rush of conscientious bishops, peers, knights and burgesses to Westminster; or that most of them were politically aware, anxious to reform the commonweal, purify religion, criticise and obstruct royal policies, and demand redress before supply. The reality was much more prosaic. Growing competition for borough seats, for example, had little to do with the rise of the Commons or increasing discontent, but much to do with local, social and economic considerations. Indebted gentlemen took advantage of the parliamentary privilege of freedom from arrest in order to savour, for a brief season, the delights which the capital had to offer, to pursue law suits in the central courts of Westminster and to secure the passage of their parliamentary bills, without harassment from their London creditors. The Queen and her Council were well aware of the irresponsible, selfish and even frivolous reasons why such men were elected [*Doc. 15*]. So too was the experienced member who wrote to a Privy Councillor in 1572, warning him that, in particular, men chosen for the first time 'are commonly . . . gladdest of large [long] parliaments to learn and see fashions' [1 *fol. 32*]. In other words, many borough members used the occasion for non-parliamentary purposes. However, extra-mural priorities and therefore absenteeism were not confined to this group. Indeed, endemic absenteeism was a general and continuing problem. The Privy Council's prime managerial concern was not to exclude the critics of particular royal policies but to muster a sufficient presence for the effective transaction of Parliament's business.

For several reasons, the attendance record of the House of Lords continued to be superior. Many members were involved in government and were in a position to advise and even influence royal policies. In other words, they were politically interested and active. Furthermore, bishops and peers constituted a small group of life-members who were acquainted with each other, the Court and the Council. They received individual writs of summons and had not only the right but also the duty to attend. If a member wished to stay away for the session, he had to apply for a royal licence and then, if successful, name one or more proctors who would speak for him and, at the same time, commit him to decisions taken in his absence [*Doc. 16*]. The proctor's authority to act rested on a written proxy which was despatched to the Clerk of the Parliaments. And the Clerk was careful to record it in his journal because this act of registration entitled him to a fee. His registration record, together with his daily attendance register, enabled the Council to monitor unauthorised absenteeism, especially as the Clerk's personal journal evolved into the Lords' official record.

Nevertheless, absenteeism persisted, with or without permission. In 1559 almost half the members of the Lords sued out licences. However, this was an exceptional Parliament, which had the task of enacting a new religious settlement, and many peers preferred circumspection, until they knew the Queen's mind and Parliament's decisions. Thereafter sessional absentees were fewer but, for a variety of reasons such as age, sickness, royal service, distance, personal distractions and simple lack of interest, there were always some – more than twenty, for example, in 1584 and 1589. Furthermore, there was no guarantee that those who turned up would attend regularly, and the daily presence occasionally thinned to fifteen or even less. This was unusual, however, and the Lords was normally served by sufficient experienced hands to perform its functions efficiently. In a small assembly of men who sat in strict order of precedence, absences were unlikely to go unnoticed by Councillors, who could also consult the Clerk's attendance register.

There is no doubt that Burghley perused the journal. In 1597 he reported to the House that the Clerk's journal books 'seemed to have some error in them, in misplacing the lords'. He successfully moved that, in future, they should be 'viewed and perused every Parliament, by certain lords of the House, to be appointed for that purpose' [15, II *p. 195*]. Four days later, again on Burghley's initiative, the House resolved that members who stayed away during the session should be admonished [*Doc. 17*]. It was difficult for delinquents to escape the watchful eye of the Council.

Absenteeism was a more serious, indeed intractable, problem in the Commons. The Lower House could not be subjected to the managerial controls which operated in the Lords, because the membership was bigger, there were not so many familiar faces and members did not sit in designated places. Moreover, for these reasons, the Underclerk could not compile an attendance record, to which Councillors might refer in order to chart the incidence of absenteeism and identify persistent offenders. In the same way historians have to depend upon snippets of information in order to identify and measure the magnitude of the problem. And certainly there was a problem. The only continuous evidence of this is to be found in the journal, when the House divided on a bill and the Clerk recorded those who voted for and against it. Supporters of the bill, the 'ayes', left the chamber whilst opponents, 'the noes', were counted in their seats by tellers whom the Speaker had appointed. Then, as the ayes returned, they too were totted up. No allowance was made for abstentions. Therefore the Clerk's record of division figures is also a complete record of the Commons' presence on those occasions. The figures are revealing. The presence during six divisions in 1563 ranged between 276 and 131, in a house of 422 members, and averaged 213 (just over 50 per cent); a mere 35 per cent divided on four occasions in 1566; in 1581 a bill narrowly passed by 98 to 89, when almost three-fifths of the members were absent; 210, 138 and a mere 78 were counted by tellers on three occasions in 1589; and in 1601 there was an average turn-out of only 44 per cent.

It is possible of course that the Council was less concerned with efficiency than the duty of duly elected members to attend. After all, so far as we can tell, numbers rarely fell below 150. On paper at least there were always enough knights and burgesses present to carry on business. However, in an assembly of amateur legislators, many of whom had not sat before, it was imperative that some of the old parliament-hands, together with the lawyers who were the skilled parliamentary draftsmen, should turn up regularly. But lawyers were enticed away from the unprofitable and tedious business of legislation by the prospect of fat fees to be made in the central law courts, which were also housed in Westminster Palace [*Doc. 18*]. Indeed, they were notorious absentees and the popular butt of contemporary jokes [*Doc. 19*]. One thing is clear, despite the patchy, often fragmentary, nature of the evidence, and that is the Council's concern to maximise attendance. Such concern was expressed in a number of ways. The Speaker continued to license members who sought early leave – for example, eighteen in 1559, thirty-three in 1566–67, and six in 1571. Their reasons (or excuses) sound plausible enough: on 'special business', royal service, 'great', 'weighty', 'urgent' or 'necessary affairs', or, more specifically, gout, a wife's sickness, an uncle's death, or the assizes. However, if the Clerk was not extraordinarily lax in recording licences, then it is clear that most intended absentees just did not bother to apply to the Speaker. A more effective way of identifying delinquents was to call the roll of members, as was done seven times in 1566–67 and 1581. When, in 1601, the House neglected to order a roll call, William Wiseman pointed out that this 'was not yet done' [20 *p. 269*].

Frequently, the Commons imposed financial penalties on defaulters [*Doc. 20*] and in April 1559 it (or the Council) resorted to extreme measures with a bill 'touching knights and burgesses, for attendance in the parliament' [21, I *p. 60*]. This proceeded no further, however, even though on the same day, 17 April, only 224 voted on another bill, a week later 131 divided, whilst on 1 May the House had shrunk to 114. Absenteeism was understandable. How could the tedium and grinding legislative process compete with the seductive pleasures of London? The Clerk's occasional journal entry was a commentary on one of the Privy Council's most serious and perennial problems. On 3 April 1559, in mid-session, he noted that 'this day Mr. Speaker, with few of this house, were here'. In 1581 'the number of them was not great', even on the opening day, though he tried to explain this away by the deaths amongst incumbent members since the previous session of 1576, the many prorogations since then and the fact that new members could not take their seats until they had sworn the oath of allegiance [21, I *pp. 59, 115–16*]. Despite the Clerk's explanation, endemic absenteeism was a harsh reality with which the conciliar managers of the Commons had to live. It was all very well for Sir Robert Cecil to commend the Commons in 1601, saying 'I am glad to see the parliament so full, which used towards the end to grow thin'. Yet he uttered those words just after a division in which 312 members had voted and just under one-third were absent [20 *p. 301*]. The fact remains that the absenteeism of knights and burgesses frustrated all official attempts to eliminate or minimise it.

6 THE POLITICAL HISTORY OF ELIZABETHAN PARLIAMENTS

Parliamentary opposition to Tudor government was always possible and it sometimes occurred, especially in an age of ideological warfare, when Catholics and Protestants persecuted and destroyed each other, and when zealots tried to impose their opinions on more moderate, compromising co-religionists. However, criticism and opposition could also be secular-based and concerned with such mundane matters as administrative abuses by royal servants. Purveyance and pre-emption – the Crown's right to purchase foodstuffs and requisition transport for the royal household, at rates arbitrarily fixed by civil servants and invariably below the current market price – engendered discontent which was frequently voiced in parliaments, especially in 1589 [92]. So too did monopolies in the closing years of Elizabeth's reign. No one questioned the monarch's right to grant a patent for an invention. It protected the inventor by granting him a monopoly to manufacture and market his new product. However, during the 1590s the Queen, desperately short of money and conducting a war on many fronts, sought ways of supplementing her shrinking patronage resources on the cheap. One device was the grant of monopolies to courtiers and royal servants, empowering them to corner the market in the manufacture, sale or licensing of a particular commodity. In 1597 there were parliamentary rumblings, to which Elizabeth responded with grace, charm and unfulfilled promises of reform. By 1601 the rumblings had become an uproar and, belatedly, she was forced to act. The Commons could also be stirred by heavy-handed officialdom trampling on precious parliamentary privileges. Any of these issues could produce a collective rush of blood to the head.

PARLIAMENTARY DYNAMICS: SIR JOHN NEALE

With this in mind it is important to remember that revisionists are in constant danger of distorting the truth about Elizabethan parliaments, especially if they deny that political conflicts could and did occur, and instead reduce parliamentary activity to nothing more than petty issues of a local, personal or sectional kind, devoid of either policy or principle. On the other hand, the Neale–Notestein interpretation elevated and inflated political conflict over matters of great moment to a central and unjustified position in the parliamentary history of the reign. It would be wrong-headed to ignore the possibility that there was an element of truth in their writings. Neale in particular was persuasive. He postulated two related and dynamic developments in the Elizabethan House of Commons. One, spawned by the Reformation, was the emergence of a persistent, troublesome, radical Protestant (Puritan) opposition. It was novel because it was organised. Its members were involved in pre-session planning, the rehearsal of tactics, and communication with radical clergy outside Parliament. Furthermore, another novelty, it was not a mere negative opposition, which sought simply to obstruct or frustrate royal policies. It was positive, with an alternative parliamentary programme of its own [72, I *p. 28*].

This organised party, the 'Puritan choir', was identified and its activities charted by Neale. In 1566–67 and 1571 the objectives of the 'choir' were to push the 'halfly-reformed' Church of the Elizabethan Settlement further down the road to the pure, reformed Church of John Calvin's Geneva, cleanse it of its surviving popish remnants and rags and upgrade its standards. However, if Elizabeth suddenly died, all of its Protestant hopes and aspirations would be destroyed by the half-French and Catholic Mary Stuart, her legitimate successor. Therefore in 1563 and 1566–67 it strove to persuade the Queen to marry and beget children or to name a reliable Protestant as her heir. It was an ambitious programme, which failed only because of her obstinacy. Then, in the 1570s, there emerged a younger, uncompromising generation of radicals. Under the leadership of Thomas Cartwright, John Field, Walter Travers and Thomas Wilcox they spurned the veteran Puritans as men who had become soft and accepted the established Church in its present condition. They rejected not only the prayer book, 'culled and picked out of that popish dunghill, the mass book', but also the office of bishop, and they even cast doubts on the legitimacy of the royal governorship. This new breed of Presbyterian Puritans blew their first trumpet blast against the monstrous regiment of bishops when they produced their two *Admonitions to the Parliament* in 1572. These were, in fact, propaganda pieces designed for a wider public than members of the Lords and Commons. Thereafter their attack was a two–pronged one. They attempted to convert or subvert the Church from within through the prophesyings and the classical movement [90 *pp. 168–79, 208–21, 296–302, 333–82*] and, at the same time, they sought instant statutory solutions through parliaments. In 1584 Dr Peter Turner inaugurated the 'bill and book' campaign. The bill, which had been 'framed by certain godly and learned ministers', would have replaced the Anglican prayer book with the Genevan liturgy (the *Form of Prayers*), and episcopal government with pastors, lay elders and assemblies. Their failure left the Presbyterians undaunted. In 1586–87 Anthony Cope's book was a revised version of the Genevan prayer book, whilst his bill would have abolished the existing Church courts, episcopate and even the royal governorship and erected a Presbyterian Church in its place. Like its predecessor, Cope's bill and book did not run the course [*Doc. 21*], and thereafter the Presbyterian cause in both Parliament and Church gradually fizzled out.

Organised Puritanism was one of Neale's parliamentary dynamics. The other, which also manifested itself in the Commons, was the growing influx of educated, self-confident gentlemen. This was a parliamentary consequence of their invasion of the universities and inns of court. In 1563 one-third of members had attended one or the other or both, and the proportion steadily rose: to 48 per cent in 1584 and 54 per cent in 1593 [71 *pp. 302–8*]. Although only a minority took a degree or were called to the Bar as lawyers, this did not necessarily mean that they treated higher education lightly, as a social rather than an academic exercise. The Tudor state required practical skills in its servants, and more and more men of noble or gentle birth, as well as careerists of humbler origins, responded to this demand. According to Neale the process had two important effects on the Commons. It was well served with lawyers and gentlemen with some legal knowledge: altogether 108 (26 per cent) in 1563, 164 (36 per cent) in 1584, and 197 (44 per cent) in 1593. They were vital in the process of drafting and revising proposed laws. Secondly, as the universities shifted their emphasis from the training of clergy to the preparation of future lay governors, they gave more attention to the practical needs of the latter – in particular the study of rhetoric – whilst moots (the hearing of imaginary cases in a mock court) and other oral exercises were an integral part of legal training. The result was, in Neale's words, 'a high standard of parliamentary oratory' [71 *pp. 307–8*].

Neale painted a glowing picture of the quality of the Elizabethan Commons:

Birth and education, expert knowledge, practical experience, and corporate solidarity – all were present in abundant measure. . . . The house of commons reached maturity in Elizabeth's reign. The instrument was tempered with which the crown was to be resisted and conquered. [71 *pp. 319–20*]

Thus he associated the improved quality of its membership with its increasing capacity and willingness to challenge royal government. The new breed of educated, skilled and self-confident gentlemen reinforced the Commons' assertiveness as it rose to parity with the Lords in the 1530s and thereafter displaced it as the more important chamber. It became increasingly sensitive of its growing stature and authority, prickly about its dignity and aggressive over the personal privileges of its members and its liberties as a house. During the sixteenth century it acquired control over the attendance, membership qualifications and discipline of its members. Chancery's customary right to resolve disputed elections was challenged. Outsiders who offended against the Commons' dignity or the privileges of those who sat there were punished: they included strangers present in the House, those who abused or assaulted members, or pages misbehaving on the stairs outside [*Doc. 22*]. In 1571 the House went further and successfully clamoured for the return of a member who had been sequestered by the Privy Council.

More important, indeed a serious challenge to personal monarchy, was the Commons' claim to an enlargement of its liberties. The crucial one was that of free speech. Elizabeth's insistence that parliaments could discuss only matters placed before them, and her obstinate and unbending position on this point, produced two Puritan – and Nealean – heroes, Paul and Peter Wentworth. When, in 1566, she forbade further discussion on her marriage and the succession, Paul asked the Commons whether she had breached its liberty of free speech. Ten years later, Peter lamented inhibiting rumours about her opinions on matters before the House, and messages, 'either of commanding or inhibiting, very injurious unto the freedom of speech and consultation' (see *Doc. 26* pp. 113–15). The Wentworths were, to Neale at least, heroic figures who struck blows for freedom and were standard-bearers in the Commons' upward march. 'Here was something fundamental: an innovation in parliamentary tactics; dawn of a new age; harbinger of Stuart conflicts' [72, I *pp. 152, 319–20*]. Neither Elizabeth's success in maintaining her restrictive interpretation of free speech, nor the Wentworth brothers' failure to demolish those restrictions affected Neale's veneration for such men, who stood in the vanguard of the advance towards the eventual triumph of parliaments. They fitted neatly into his overall picture of parliamentary development: an institution growing in authority; a House of Commons politically maturing and increasing its power, improving its quality, extending its privileges and liberties, and displaying greater ability and preparedness to challenge royal authority – all steps along the highroad to civil war.

PARLIAMENTARY OPPOSITION: THE REVISIONISTS' VIEW

Revisionists have questioned and modified this picture in several important particulars, chiefly because they have a different way of looking at things. They are institutionally rather than politically oriented. Therefore they are more concerned to examine the mechanics of parliaments, how they carried out their essential law-making function, rather than to seek out moments of high drama and crisis. This does not guarantee a more accurate history of Elizabethan parliaments. Nevertheless, the revisionist treatment has one particular strength, that it rests upon a comprehensive institutional analysis rather than a selective study of political episodes. As a result, apparently sinister political moves, either to manipulate Parliament or to challenge the Queen's authority, are seen for what they really were: as procedural innovations designed to improve efficiency for example, or as normal business routines (see pp. 68–9). If it is remembered that parliaments were called to assist royal government, that, for the most part, the reign was characterised by harmony between the Crown and the governing class, and that parliaments reflected that relationship, then much else falls into place. This is particularly true of the history of parliamentary privilege and liberties and of the incidence of conflict and opposition. The orthodox historians related these as parts of one historical process, the political rise of the House of Commons. In contrast, the institutional analysis of the revisionists identifies the growth of privilege and liberties as institutional improvements in the efficiency of parliaments. And this applied especially to the Commons, which had much ground to make up on its older partner, the Lords. In the same way the revisionists' study of parliamentary business places conflict in a more realistic perspective. It was not the norm, nor even a common occurrence, but an infrequent episode in a general climate of co-operation. This is not, however, to belittle the significance of disagreements, heated debates and conflicts, when they occurred. After all, the issues which engendered them – succession, the reformation of religion, the Catholic threat and government malpractices – were of major importance to members of the governing élite.

PARLIAMENTARY PRIVILEGES

The history of the privilege of freedom from arrest, for example, could be regarded as symptomatic of the maturation and rise of the Commons. However, that would amount to a misreading of the facts. Already an old and well-established privilege by the sixteenth century, it simply protected members from private actions at law during a parliamentary session. Almost every privilege case in the Elizabethan Commons concerned parliamentary knights or burgesses who were in debt to London merchants, financiers, or money-lenders. Their arrival in the metropolis provided their creditors with an opportunity to take steps to recover their money. However, knights and burgesses were coming on the Queen's business – to sit in her Parliament – and this was deemed to take precedence over the lawsuits of her subjects. To this extent it was a practical and sensible privilege, because it enabled them to carry out their parliamentary duties without let or hindrance. Perhaps with less justification this privilege had been extended to the servants of members, because – so the argument ran – they would be unable to fulfil their responsibilities adequately without them.

Although this privilege was not a Tudor innovation, there was a significant change in its enforcement during the sixteenth century. Until Ferrers's case in 1542 it had been the Lord Chancellor's right and responsibility to release a member or his servant, who had been arrested for debt at the suit of his creditors, but in that year the Commons acted on its own authority to release George Ferrers and continued to do so thereafter. This was not done in defiance of the Crown, but with the explicit approval of Henry VIII (see p. 13), and his successors did not question the Commons' right to enforce the privilege. However, it was open to abuse. Debtors could enjoy the pleasures of London without fear of molestation and, if their creditors were foolish enough to act, they (or their imprisoned servants) could plead privilege. The House would free them and punish both the creditors and the officers of the law who had seized them and so committed a breach of privilege [*Doc. 23*]. Furthermore, a member imprisoned for a debt and then released could not be arrested again for the same debt. The Queen and her close servants did not question the privilege, but criticised its abuse. In 1571 she noted how some members were elected in order to avoid legal action during their stay in London [*Doc. 15*]. Perhaps Lord Keeper Puckering echoed this sentiment in 1593 when, in response to the petition of the Commons' Speaker for the customary privileges, he said that freedom of arrest 'might be cautiously made use of' [*7 pp. 469–70*]. Official concern was certainly justified. The Lower House was inclined to be self-indulgent in this matter, with the result that creditors were sometimes penalised for pursuing their just rights, whilst debtors went scot-free.

On the other hand, the Commons did not always and automatically throw the mantle of its corporate privilege over knights and burgesses who had been arrested. It was capable of discriminating, judging cases on their merits, and even deciding against one of its own members [*Doc. 24*]. The most notable occasion was when in 1576 it balked at the trickery of Arthur Hall, the choleric and mentally unstable burgess for Grantham in Lincolnshire. Hall had already incurred the displeasure of the House with a speech sympathetic to Mary Stuart in 1572. He challenged the demand of that ardent anti-Catholic, Thomas Norton, for her execution, but 'the house misliked so much of his talk that, with shuffling of feet and hawking, they had well nigh barred him to be heard' [*2 fol. 54*]. On that occasion he was called to the bar to answer for his intemperate speech, and he submitted without grace. Sir Francis Knollys, Treasurer of the Household, advised the Commons that 'he lacketh discretion and therefore wise men may the rather bear with him. His father before him [was] somewhat inclined to madness [and one of his sons was mentally retarded]. He would have him condemned for a rash head and a fool' [*6 fol. 28; 79, II p. 240*]. When, in 1576, Hall's servant, Edward Smalley, was arrested, convicted and fined £100 for an assault on his master's enemy Melchisedech Mallory, the member for Grantham moved for his release. The Commons' members suspected an attempt to abuse parliamentary privilege, none more so than Thomas Norton and his friend, colleague and Recorder of London, William Fleetwood. Smalley was released from his London prison, only to be consigned to the Tower by the Commons, until he paid his debt. The House then censured both master and servant [*8 p. 262; 72, I pp. 338–40; 94 p. 88*]. If the Smalley case has a niche in the history of parliamentary privilege, its place in the 1576 session ought not to be exaggerated. It occupied the time of the House, and then by no means all of the time, on only eight of its thirty-nine sittings.

Although Tudor monarchs sensibly protected the Commons' privilege of freedom from arrest in civil suits, in the cause of efficient parliaments, there were limits beyond which it could not proceed. In 1585 the House asserted its 'ancient privileges' to prevent members being served with a subpoena (a writ which ordered a defendant or witness to appear in a law court) during the Parliament time. The Lord Chancellor denied its claim unless it could produce precedents 'allowed and ratified' in the Queen's law courts [7 *p. 347*]. The Commons searched unsuccessfully for such precedents and did not pursue the matter. Nor did it protest when, in 1593, one of its burgesses, Thomas Fitzherbert, was arrested by the Crown for debts amounting to £1,400 [79, II *p. 125*]. In contrast, it did act successfully in 1589 to prevent members from being called away to lawsuits which had been transferred from the central courts at Westminster to the assizes (periodic sessions presided over by central-court judges in the counties). None of this amounted to a conscious attempt to enlarge privilege, but simply to prevent the depletion of its membership [7 *p. 436*].

However, the Crown's removal or imprisonment of a member for an offence committed in the House was a different matter. Such a political reprisal was liable to provoke an uproar. This happened when the Privy Council ordered William Strickland to stay away during the 1571 session, after he had introduced a bill to revise the book of common prayer, contrary to the Queen's command not to meddle in religious matters [72 *pp. 200–3*]. This case concerned two related problems: Elizabeth's novel restraints on what Parliament might discuss (see pp. 49–51) and uncertainty as to what she could legitimately do when someone breached these restraints. The Queen was compelled to back down and restore Strickland. Thereafter she was more circumspect and prepared the ground carefully: so the Presbyterian agitators in 1586–87 and Peter Wentworth, who intended to move for a settlement of the succession in 1593, were arrested for extra-parliamentary activities which were not covered by privilege.

PARLIAMENTARY LIBERTIES

Whereas privileges protected individuals in the performance of their parliamentary duties, liberties enabled the two houses to carry out their vital taxative, legislative and advisory functions [8 *pp. 260–8*]. In several respects the Tudor Commons enlarged its liberties. It acquired the right to decide the qualifications of membership (for example, in 1550 and 1553), to adjudicate on disputed elections (from 1586 onwards), to regulate attendance (by an Act of 1515 which authorised the Speaker to license absences), and to censure or punish outsiders. It also disciplined its own members for offences committed in the House. It sent Peter Wentworth to the Tower for offensive speech against the Queen in 1576, and it placed Dr Parry in custody in 1584 for accusing members of promoting terror, victimisation and 'their own greedy desires' when they passed the bill against Jesuits [79, III *p. 182*]. In 1581 it went further when it fined, imprisoned and, for the first time, expelled one of its number, Arthur Hall, for an offence committed outside its walls. Angry about his treatment in 1576, Hall had written a tract which criticised some members, including Speaker Bell and Thomas Norton, and, more important, provocatively but accurately investigated the antiquity of Parliament. Conducting himself like a good revisionist historian, Hall examined its history in terms of its purpose: its vital legislative function. He dismissed the pretentious claims that it had existed 'time out of mind', traced its origins accurately to the thirteenth century, and concluded 'that the Lower House was a new person in the Trinity'. This conclusion gave great offence to some of its influential members. Moreover, when he had a small edition printed – at the most eighty to a hundred copies – he publicised the secret proceedings of the Commons.

Thus far it seems to be a straightforward enough story. Hall was punished for offending the dignity and pretensions of a self-important and power-conscious House, as well as impugning the reputation of particular members [72, 1 *pp. 407–10*; 97 *pp. 356, 359–63*]. Elton, however, introduced a new, complex and significant dimension to the Hall case, when he linked it to the ongoing Privy Council debate on the Anjou match [94 *pp. 91–7*]. This was Elizabeth's projected marriage to the French Catholic duc d'Anjou. The 'on-off' courtship had commenced in 1572, lapsed, revived in 1573, and again in 1578 – this time over an extended period to the end of 1581. During the years 1578–81, the Queen publicly displayed enthusiasm, but conciliar support for the marriage declined. Whereas Lord Treasurer Burghley at first represented a considerable body of conciliar opinion in favour of the union, a number of Councillors changed their minds. In 1579 Sir Walter Mildmay, who was consistently opposed to the alliance, was joined by the Earl of Leicester and Sir Christopher Hatton. By 1581 proponents of the match, including Burghley, were only a minority of the Privy Council.

Arthur Hall's protector and one-time guardian was the Lord Treasurer, who in 1581 strove to save him from his own follies. It was Elton's belief that the parliamentary hunt for Hall's disgrace was dictated by conciliar divisions rather than by the outraged sensibilities of the House of Commons. The Privy Councillors, such as Hatton, Mildmay and Secretary Wilson, who played leading roles in the proceedings against Burghley's ex-ward, were opposed to the Anjou marriage [Doc. 25]. When the anti-marriage faction struck at Hall, they were actually aiming at Burghley. In Elton's view, the episode had little, if anything, to do with a sensitive, self-conscious, politically assertive Commons, but was, rather, a classic example of the covert way in which Elizabethan conciliar factions exploited parliaments for their own ends [94]. The role of Thomas Norton, however, raises some doubts about this explanation of the Hall affair. It was Norton who drew the Commons' attention to the printed libel and so initiated parliamentary proceedings against its author. His animosity was understandable and predictable for a number of reasons: Hall had expressed sympathy for Catholicism and Rome; in his printed pamphlet he had 'defamed the memory' of some of Norton's parliamentary colleagues (including his friend the late Robert Bell, Speaker in 1576), impugned the authority of the House and published its secret proceedings. The long-standing antagonism between the two men, for these and other reasons, and extending back to Hall's sympathetic support for Mary Stuart in 1572, suffice to explain Norton's active role. But it is improbable that he would have willingly supported or allowed himself to be used in a scheme designed to bring about Burghley's public discomfiture. The Lord Treasurer was the chief patron of Norton, whose devotion and service to him had been long and unswerving [97 *pp. 355–63*]. As for the Councillors who were active in the Hall affair, Mildmay appears to have been genuinely offended by Hall's attack on the House and on some of its members. Secretary Wilson was one of those criticised in the libel. And Hatton, who reported to the House on Hall's examination by a Commons' committee, was impatient to wind up the business so that time could be spent in 'matters of greatest moment' [21 *p. 125*]. The hostile response of a sensitive assembly remains the probable explanation for the activity of these Councillors and of devoted House of Commons men such as Norton.

As a postscript, it should be noted that, Hall apart, the Commons censured or punished members only for their activities in the House. Furthermore, it might commit an offender to prison, but the Crown alone could release or pardon him [65 *p. 86*]. So Hall's fine and imprisonment were remitted as soon as Parliament had been dissolved, presumably at Burghley's suit [94 *pp. 95–7*].

The most important liberty of each house was freedom of speech. It was crucial to the effective functioning of parliaments. If they were to perform their essential legislative and advisory responsibilities properly, their members had to be free to speak their minds without fear of reprisals from other subjects or from the Queen herself. In practice, there had been a degree of free speech long before the first recorded formal request by the Speaker (Sir Thomas More) in his opening address in 1523. Neither then nor afterwards was unrestricted freedom sought or granted: simply that members might voice their opinions freely, but without offensive speech, and then only on matters placed before them, not on any subject of their choice. However, regular requests and grants in the many parliaments of the Reformation, between 1529 and 1559, transformed such grants from acts of royal grace into a mere formal acknowledgment of parliamentary rights – at least, that is how some Elizabethan members saw this liberty.

In fact, the question whether the traditional, restricted version of free speech was a matter of grace or right was not raised in the Elizabethan parliaments. Disagreements occurred about the restraints. Elizabeth maintained a consistent position, distinguishing between matters of commonweal and state. The former encompassed not only general social and economic measures, touching the entire community, but also the many sectional, local and personal bills submitted to parliaments. These could be introduced without the Crown's prior consent and freely discussed. In contrast, the two houses could debate only those affairs of state placed before them. Because of Elizabeth's claim that religion was the preserve of her bishops and Convocation, her insistence that her marriage, succession and foreign policy were prerogative matters, and her reluctance to proceed harshly against Mary Stuart or the English Catholics, she was unwilling to allow discussion of them. Yet those were precisely the issues which concerned so many loyal, responsible, Protestant members of the governing class, Privy Councillors amongst them. Indeed, the Queen, not the Commons, was the innovator. She changed the direction of royal government. Until 1559 the Crown had provided the dynamic of leadership and dramatic alteration in religious and secular affairs. Thereafter it became a conservative bulwark, the obstinate defender of the *status quo*, resisting both the dangerous forces of further change and sensible moves to protect the state and new national Church. It should be emphasised that this was a particular problem for the Lower House, because bishops and nobles, with their many lines of communication into the Court, had other and extra-parliamentary ways of influencing the royal decision-making process. The only practical solution for many politically concerned knights and burgesses was to remove the existing restraints on free speech because, without full and frank discussion of urgent matters, they could not be brought to a satisfactory legislative solution.

Logic and recent history supported this point of view. Writs of summons to the lords spiritual and temporal called them specifically to counsel the Queen on religion and defence of the realm, and this advisory role was not exclusive to the Lords. Henry VIII had permitted wide-ranging criticisms of his policies without taking drastic reprisals. Henrician, Edwardian and Marian changes in religion had been promoted by the state and enacted by parliaments, often after lengthy and searching debate in both houses. That was true of the Elizabethan Settlement too. After all, it was a traditional function of parliaments to proffer advice to the monarch, even when it was unsolicited and perhaps unwelcome. After 1559, however, Elizabeth attempted to stem and indeed reverse the tide of recent parliamentary history, when she imposed new restraints and employed intimidatory practices to which her father, for example, had not resorted. According to Peter Wentworth, she was informed of the Commons' proceedings, not only by Privy Councillors (who, after all, were simply doing their duty), but also by ingratiating, tell-tale courtiers. The Queen then used such information, circulating rumours of her displeasure, despatching stern messages and handing down prohibitions on discussion.

Although the Wentworth brothers, Paul and Peter, were not alone in their attempts to defend free speech, they certainly took the lead. However, like the Queen, they adopted a novel interpretation. They demanded, as a matter of right, full, free and unrestricted discussion on all subjects, not merely those which she placed before parliaments. Paul Wentworth raised the issue of free speech in 1566 and Peter did so in 1571, 1576 and 1587. However, the Commons' response to Paul was a mixed one; in 1576 it sent Peter to the Tower for commencing a speech which contained offensive remarks about the Queen; and in 1587 she imprisoned him during the session, without provoking widespread protest in the House [*Doc. 26*]. Despite such actions, Elizabeth did not succeed in imposing her definition of limited free speech on her parliaments. In the Parliament of 1563–66/67 the Commons debated the need for a settled succession and petitioned her to this end. Repeatedly thereafter, such important issues as religious reformation, the elimination of administrative abuses, anti-Catholic legislation, and the problem of Mary Stuart were raised and discussed. Sometimes her peremptory prohibitions put an end to debate, but she could not prevent the initial airing of such matters. Nor did her imperious commands make the problems go away.

In their efforts to free the Commons from the narrow constraints of Elizabeth's control, the Wentworths could be foolhardy, impetuous and politically inept. Peter, in particular, contributed nothing to the productivity and efficiency of the Commons. Although he was one of Neale's parliamentary heroes, he was, in terms of revisionist priorities, little more than a parliamentary nuisance [*96 p. 29; 8 p. 267; 72*]. Nevertheless, the Wentworths were not simply mavericks, isolated from the mainstream of parliamentary opinion. Some of the particular causes which Peter pursued, such as the advancement of Presbyterianism, enjoyed scant support. But when he upheld the right to speak freely he was not alone [68]. MacCaffrey argues that, when the Lower House sought to extend freedom of discussion from commonwealth to prerogative concerns, it was attempting 'to gain control of the whole agenda of the House' [*70 p. 146*]. This was not Neale's rising Commons, throwing out challenges to the Crown's authority. Rather, it reflected the response of members to pressing problems, to a restrictive monarch and to the growing acceptance that Parliament was both the national debating forum and natural counsel to the Queen. Nevertheless, those who were bold or foolish enough to trespass on forbidden territory continued to pay the penalty. In 1593 James Morrice, one of Burghley's subordinate officials, launched a parliamentary attack on Archbishop Whitgift in the Commons. He was placed under house arrest and his career prospects were irreparably damaged. The Queen said that his disloyalty to her, in criticising her archbishop 'should be a bar against any preferment at her hands' [*79, 3 p. 99*]. Nevertheless, there were always men like Morrice or the Wentworths, who, in the Commons, would display a mixture of loyalty, independence, and a willingness to overstep the mark in order to speak their minds.

The Elizabethan history of Commons' liberties and privileges was not one of deliberate, planned political advancement, but rather one of institutional improvement, enabling it to perform its legislative and counselling functions more effectively. In the earlier parliaments of the reign the House was dealing in matters of privilege, membership and elections by the use of *ad hoc* committees. In each of the next three parliaments, in 1584/85, 1586/87 and 1589, it established a select committee for privileges. Then, in 1593 (and in the last two Elizabethan parliaments), one such committee was charged with responsibility for both privileges and election returns. These developments were accompanied by occasional clashes with successive Lord Chancellors over the respective authority of Crown and Commons – indeed, in 1586 the Queen accused the House of 'impertinent' interference in matters pertaining to the office of Lord Chancellor. These were not, however, the consequences of some concerted attempt by the Commons to 'win the initiative' or to create political confrontation with the government. The committees of 1593–1601 invariably included all the Privy Councillors and Crown legal officers who were members of the House. And in 1601 an *ad hoc* committee was also appointed for the purpose of consultation with Lord Keeper Egerton [81].

What happened in the Lower House must be seen in the context of Parliament as a whole. The Lords was more self-assured about its liberties and seemingly unaware of real or imagined threats to them. So, in the 1590s, Richard Robinson could write that their lordships 'have also freedom of speech granted everyone of them to speak his mind boldly' [18 *p. 10*]. However, the Upper House was just as sensitive about the privileges of its members. In 1572 Henry Lord Cromwell complained to the Lords that his arrest, by order of the Court of Chancery in the previous year, was 'contrary to the ancient privilege and immunity, time out of memory, unto the lords of parliament and peers of this realm'. The House rejected Lord Keeper Bacon's defence of Chancery, of which he was the presiding officer. After consultation with its legal assistants, it concluded that there were no precedents for the attachment (arrest) of 'any lord, having place and voice in parliament' and so discharged Cromwell [78]. However, the Lords added an important and reasonable general qualification when it ruled that if, in the future, a peer's attachment was found to be justified, then it should remain in force [78 *p. 13*]. In 1584, too, common sense and moderation prevailed when the House refused Viscount Bindon's request for privilege for his servant, on the grounds that 'he was not a menial servant, nor yet ordinary attendant' upon him [7 *p. 315*]. The Elizabethan history of privilege in both houses was one of a tendency to self-indulgence, tempered by a certain reasonableness and a sense of natural justice. Certainly it is not the story of a concerted Commons' campaign to enlarge its freedom of action and throw off the shackles of royal control.

PARLIAMENTARY DYNAMICS: SIR JOHN NEALE RECONSIDERED

Nor does the record of crisis, conflict and opposition in the Lower House point to its political maturation and rise. Norman Jones's close scrutiny of the 1559 Parliament destroyed the ghostly battalion of Puritan activists who flitted through Neale's account of the Elizabethan Settlement [101 *pp. 63–72*]. Thereafter Neale's twin dynamics of the Commons' advancement – educated gentry and religious radicalism – have been disproved or at least re-assessed. He was undoubtedly right about the invasion of the house by carpet-bagging gentlemen, a large number of whom had been schooled at university and/or inn of court [71 *pp. 302–8*]. However, this was the continuation of a process which was already under way in the early fifteenth century. In any case, many of them were returned by the nomination or through the influence of noble patrons. This was a circumstance which did less to reinforce the Commons than to augment the institutional authority of the Upper House with the social and parliamentary influence of the peers who sat there [65 *pp. 80–1*; 134].

Neale's second dynamic, an organised Puritan opposition, which attempted to impose its political programme and its own vision of the godly society through Parliament, has suffered even more at the hands of his critics. He identified two phases in which moderate Puritanism in 1563, 1566–67 and 1571 progressed to Presbyterianism in 1572, 1584–85 and 1586–87. If the objectives of moderate Puritans and Presbyterians differed, their techniques did not. They were organised and their parliamentary campaigns were characterised by pre-session planning, the rehearsal of tactics, collaboration with radical clergy outside and the exploitation of wide support within the Commons. And they demanded unrestricted freedom of speech in order to further their ends through Parliament. However, Neale's thesis does not stand up to examination. His account of an organised opposition, the 'Puritan choir' in 1563 and 1566–67, was heavily reliant on an irrelevant document and the framework of supposition which he erected on it [72, I *pp. 91–2*,

95, 101–11, 134–70]. Recent research has demolished the validity of both his evidence and his assumptions, leaving only the proceedings of 1571 as possible proof of the moderate Puritans' parliamentary religious campaigns [30 *pp. 355–8; 133 pp. 12–14; 7 p. 310*]. And it is now clear that even that episode was not an example of a Puritan opposition at work, but a collaborative exercise between Councillors, bishops and other members of the governing class in Parliament [133 *pp. 12–13*]. In contrast, there is no doubt that the new generation of Presbyterian-Puritans did make concerted attempts to demolish the Elizabethan Settlement (see pp. 40–1). Their parliamentary manoeuvres in 1584 and 1587 were carefully planned and co-ordinated [72, II *pp. 62–3, 148–57*]. However, in 1584 the Commons would not agree even to read Turner's bill, and although it decided to hear Cope's measure in 1587, the Queen acted promptly and without protest in order to prevent it from proceeding. The Presbyterian campaigns were mounted by a handful of members, lacked general parliamentary sympathy or support and were easily smothered by official action.

The remaining example of an agitated House of Commons occurred with the grievance of harmful monopolies in 1597 and 1601. That it became so serious was, in large part, the Queen's fault. Monopolies were royal grants empowering specified individuals to manufacture or market particular commodities (or to license others to do so). In the 1590s the financial pressures of war compelled Elizabeth to reduce direct material rewards, such as grants and leases of land and pensions to her servants, and replace them with benefits which cost the Crown nothing. So monopolies rapidly multiplied. Thus far she could hardly be blamed, but when, in 1597, the Commons grumbled about the proliferation of monopolies, she promised reform and did nothing. In 1601 the pent-up anger of the governing class exploded in the Lower House. At last Elizabeth was obliged to act. She promised the immediate cancellation of some monopolies, the suspension of others, and that the rest would be examinable before the law courts [*Doc. 27*]. This parliamentary episode must be seen in its right perspective. Parliaments were occasions for the monarch to take counsel. Elizabeth had not heeded such counsel in 1597 and paid the price in 1601. But that was no more than the normal give-and-take of the parliamentary process. Just as the Queen or her Lord Chancellor, in her name, could admonish Parliament to spend its time on public matters of great urgency, leave aside private matters and not meddle in questions of religion, so Parliament could warn her of public unrest. The monopolies agitation was not an example of a rising House of Commons, but of rising discontent. Nor was it the consequence of an organised parliamentary opposition, Puritan or otherwise. It was a spontaneous response to a common grievance, voiced by the governing class through its representatives.

None of this denies the presence of friction, disharmony, disagreement, even conflict, in Elizabethan parliaments. The complaints, agitation, indiscretion or provocative conduct of individual members were common enough occurrences: for example, when, in 1593, Robert Beale, Clerk of the Privy Council, was reported to have opposed an increased tax grant; and when James Morrice attacked the disciplinary actions of Archbishop Whitgift and the Court of High Commission. This is hardly surprising, because parliaments were occasions when a formidable Queen met the power-conscious élites of Church and state and a competitive, acquisitive, self-confident governing class. Their arrogance, sensitivity, and self-righteous convictions were bound to bubble to the surface – and quite frequently too [65 *p. 87*]. The revisionists' argument, that Elizabeth would not have continued to summon parliaments if they proved to be consistently difficult, is unconvincing. She needed parliaments for money, if for nothing else. Elizabeth had no option but to call them. However, when she did, disagreements and differences of opinion rarely escalated into constitutional conflicts. Although she attempted to place specific subjects out of bounds, she knew, as an increasingly experienced politician, that parliaments were the appropriate occasions to air grievances, national issues, and local problems and to resolve some of the disputes between multifarious and often conflicting interests. Disagreements were normally brought to a satisfactory conclusion or kept within bounds by an essential harmony between Crown and governing class or by skilful conciliar management. As a last resort the Queen could veto unacceptable bills or defuse an explosive situation with honeyed words or well-timed concessions, such as the remission of one-third of the subsidy in 1566–67 and her action on monopolies in 1601. The central and continuing parliamentary problems of the Privy Council were not opposition and conflict in the Commons, but the latter's inefficiency (see pp. 79–84).

There was another potentially disruptive parliamentary force. In the three preceding reigns, factions in Court and Council had carried their conflicts into parliaments in order to discomfort, embarrass, or even overthrow their opponents (see pp. 15–16). When this happened it threatened unproductive, even addled, parliaments, because the Privy Council, responsible for the smooth conduct of parliamentary affairs, became instead a divided body, a divisive force and, especially in 1553–55, the catalyst of conflict. The Elizabethan Council was often divided: Burghley against Leicester; the reforming Anglicans against the disciplinarian Whitgift; the Cecilians against Essex. However, such conflicts were fought out at the Council board and in the Court, and did not spill over into Parliament, even during the bitter faction-fights of the 1590s. Elizabethan Councillors remained responsible royal servants in Parliament and, when they chose to use it as their gladiatorial arena, they did so in subtle and muted ways [65 *pp. 99–100*].

THE PARLIAMENTARY POLITICS OF THE PRIVY COUNCIL

If dynamic Puritanism, the invasion of the Commons by educated gentry, and Court-Council conflicts did not have significant parliamentary repercussions, how does one explain the succession and marriage campaigns of 1563 and 1566–67, the attempts to purify the Anglican Church (1566–67 and 1571), condemn Mary Stuart (1572), sharpen the treason laws (1571) and penalise the English Catholics, all of which encountered royal resistance? The answer lies, paradoxically, in the activities of the Queen's Privy Council, whose members swore a special oath of allegiance and were bound to serve her honestly and loyally. The Council was the linchpin of government or, in the words of Thomas Norton, 'the wheels that hold the chariot of England upright'. One of its responsibilities was parliamentary management. However, Councillors such as the Earls of Bedford, Leicester and Sussex, William Cecil, Francis Knollys, Walter Mildmay and Francis Walsingham were also members of a predominantly Protestant governing class. When their royal mistress vacillated or refused to make decisions on matters of vital concern to them, they persuaded her to call Parliament, usually or ostensibly for money, but occasionally, as in 1572 and 1586–87, to consult on great issues. Then they used such occasions to marshal support and pressurise her into action: a settled Protestant succession; punitive measures against her legitimate but Catholic heir, Mary Stuart; ecclesiastical reform; and tougher penal laws against Jesuits, seminary priests and English Catholic recusants.

Therefore it was Councillors, not members of a Puritan opposition, who used parliaments to coerce the Queen to their point of view. In 1563 Cecil's client, Thomas Norton, read aloud to the

Commons the succession petition which its committee had drafted. During the next session Cecil himself helped to draft the abortive subsidy preamble in which was included Elizabeth's promise to marry or name a successor [72, I *pp. 105, 162*]. When, in 1566–67 and 1571, Parliament considered the so-called alphabetical bills, labelled A–F, fifteen bishops petitioned the Queen in support of bill A. This gave parliamentary confirmation to the thirty-nine articles of religion as enacted by the Convocation of the clergy in 1563 [72, I *pp. 167–8; 65 pp. 83–4*]. The rest of the alphabetical bills were intended to improve the quality of the clergy. In 1566 bill A was introduced on 5 December and the rest on the following day. It was clearly an organised exercise, but the question is who organised it? According to Neale they were unofficial bills and the work of the Puritan opposition. Yet the history of bill A suggests an alternative explanation. It passed the Commons and received the bishops' strong support in the Lords. Thereupon Elizabeth intervened and ordered the House to proceed no further. It was William Cecil, hardly a member of a Puritan opposition, who noted with dismay that bill A was 'stayed, to the comfort of the adversaries' [72, I *pp. 166, 170*]. The 'adversaries' were presumably the Catholics. This would fit with the oft-repeated opinion of bishops, Councillors and their clients, especially Thomas Norton, that the best defence against the Catholic threat was a purified Anglican Church, administered by a godly, qualified clergy.

The alphabetical bills failed in 1566–67 and were re-introduced in 1571. Once again Neale – and Professor Collinson too – identified this as a pre-arranged campaign mounted by radical ministers and Puritans in the Commons [72, I *pp. 193–8; 90 pp. 116–17*]. The bald facts culled from the Commons' journal would seem to confirm this. Early in the session William Strickland addressed the House on the *Reformatio Legum Ecclesiasticarum* and the ABC bills, whereupon Norton presented them for its consideration. A few days later Strickland introduced a bill to revise the prayer book which he recommended for enactment. The *Reformatio* was a draft revision of canon law. It was the work of a committee, chaired by Thomas Cranmer, in Edward VI's reign, but it had not been adopted. As for the prayer book bill, it was designed to remove objectionable ceremonies and vestments which had survived from the pre-Reformation Church. In Collinson's view it was a Puritan programme designed to complete the reformation in doctrine, order of worship, and discipline which the Elizabeth Settlement had only begun [90 *p. 117*].

Whilst there is unmistakable evidence of pre-session planning and organisation in this campaign, Neale and Collinson were wrong about its authorship and meaning. Norton's father-in-law, Archbishop Thomas Cranmer, had bequeathed to him a copy of the *Reformatio*. It had recently been edited by John Foxe, author of the *Book of Martyrs,* and published with the approval of Elizabeth's first Archbishop of Canterbury, Matthew Parker. It suggests official sponsorship, not the work of a Puritan opposition. Furthermore, Councillors, bishops, and many other members of the Lords and Commons approved or actively assisted in the promotion of the *Reformatio* and ABC bills, but not Strickland's rash action. When he introduced the prayer book bill, he let the side down: not only his collaborator, but also Norton's conciliar patrons and episcopal allies. His move probably sabotaged the religious campaign because it presented the unsympathetic Queen with an opportunity to reject virtually the whole programme, moderate and sensible though it was, along with Strickland's more objectionable measure. Only bill B, concerning the clergy's subscription to the articles of religion, and bill E, against simony, survived to become laws [72, I *pp. 207, 217*; 133 *pp. 12–13*]. Elizabeth also vetoed the bill for 'coming to the church and receiving of the communion', which imposed a test of conscience and enjoyed episcopal, conciliar and Commons support [26 *pp. 273–4*].

In 1572 the Privy Council mounted one of its most elaborate and well-organised campaigns. Its object was to overcome the doubts and prevarication of the Queen in order to secure the deaths of Mary Stuart and the Duke of Norfolk, who had already been convicted of treason for conspiring to marry Mary and remove Elizabeth. Robert Bell, a man connected to Lord Keeper Bacon, was the Council's choice for Speaker of the Commons. In their addresses to Parliament, during the opening ceremonies, both Bacon and Bell [6 *fols 1, 3–4v*] hinted at the Council's objectives. The clients of Bacon and his ally Cecil, now elevated to the Upper House as Baron Burghley, took the cue. In debate and in committee, in the presentation of written papers to the Commons [10 *pp. 294–301*] and in joint conference with the Lords, the Council's men-of-business relentlessly pursued their quarry. Thomas Dannett (the Earl of Leicester's servant, a distant relative of Burghley and possibly Archbishop Parker's parliamentary nominee), Thomas Digges (connected to both Bacon and Leicester), Thomas Wilbraham (an official in the Court of Wards, of which Burghley was Master), Robert Newdigate (whose parliamentary patron was probably Baron

Hunsdon, Elizabeth's cousin, who favoured Norfolk's execution), the new Commons' Clerk, Fulk Onslow (who was Burghley's appointee and kept him informed of proceedings in this session), all lent their support to the incomparable Thomas Norton. He led the hunt with a dozen speeches, written arguments and his skill as a parliamentary draftsman. In the Upper House the bishops, lawyers and the judges on the woolsacks played their parts, too, in a campaign orchestrated by the Council [*Doc. 28*]. Elizabeth bowed to their pressure when, during the session, she gave them the Duke's head, but she frustrated all their attempts to destroy Mary [133 *pp. 24–9*].

Councillors lamented the folly of their royal mistress and figuratively rent their hair in frustration. Nevertheless, they persevered in their endeavours and scored some successes: with harsher penal laws against obdurate Catholic recusants (in 1581) and against Jesuits and seminary priests (1581 and 1585), the act 'for the Queen's surety' (1585) and eventually, in 1587, the cherished prize of Mary Stuart's head. However, whilst the Privy Councillors were capable of guiding, encouraging, and providing leadership, they did not control the Commons. Even when they were in harmony with the general sentiment of the House, and they were co-ordinating parliamentary pressure on the Queen, their desire not to offend her could be ignored by over-zealous members: for example, in 1566 the move to incorporate in the subsidy preamble her promise to marry and settle the succession, and the attempts to tack harsh provisions on to the bills concerning treasons (1571), Mary Stuart (1572), and slanders against the Queen in 1581 [97 *pp. 174–8, 192–3, 241*].

In keeping with Parliament's legitimate role as the great national debating forum, members also raised important issues, some of which, such as the grievances of purveyance and monopolies, were an embarrassment to Privy Councillors. Those pertaining to religion in particular could engender intense feeling, heated debate and, sometimes, royal anger. For two related reasons – because Parliament was the supreme law-making body and because Roman Catholicism had been restored by statute in Mary Tudor's reign – the new Elizabethan Anglican Church had to be established in 1559 by authority of Parliament. This virtually ended the introduction of bills of reform by the government. After 1559 such bills derived either from the Church, especially the bishops and Convocation, or from unofficial sources [104]. Some of the unofficial measures, such as the alphabetical bills in 1566 and 1571, enjoyed a favourable Commons' reception. Others, amongst them William Strickland's bill to reform the book of common prayer, and the Presbyterian bills of Dr Peter Turner (1584) and Anthony Cope (1586), do not appear to have received significant support. However, such unofficial reform measures, even the moderate ABC bills in 1566, received a similar hostile royal response. So, in 1581, did Paul Wentworth's motion for a public fast and a daily parliamentary sermon, which divided both the Council and the House. Bills and motions by men of reforming temper could also be a cause of discomfort for Privy Councillors, whose attempt to prevent Cope's bill from being read in 1586 was overriden by the Commons. On the other hand, there is no doubt that some of them favoured the ABC bills, one of which (giving statutory authority to the thirty-nine articles) passed into law in 1571.

As Norman Jones has shown, religious legislation covered a variety of different, though interrelated, concerns: such as the worship, discipline, structure and ecclesiastical property of the Anglican Church; penal laws against the religious enemies of that Church and the state, in particular the Catholics; and the application of religious standards to economic, social and moral matters, such as usury, Sunday activities and witchcraft [102; 104]. The regular reappearance of religious issues and legislative proposals is not surprising in an age of religious intensity, in which Protestantism and the state were inseparable to men of the Elizabethan parliaments.

Some issues of major political importance – in particular the succession, the Queen's marriage and the menace of Mary Stuart – also tended to be raised in one Parliament after another. It is convenient to criticise Elizabeth for her inaction, which prolonged the parliamentary life of such issues. However, to name a successor was to create a reversionary interest and to eliminate Mary might provoke military reprisals from the Catholic powers. The Queen's 'obstinacy' could more accurately be described as her political and diplomatic skill and flexibility. In any case, Mary's death in 1587 removed one major issue. As Elizabeth passed beyond child-bearing age, marriage gradually ceased to be a matter of parliamentary debate – though in 1576 she was still being petitioned by the Commons on the subject. A settled succession, too, seems to have lost some of the urgency with which it was invested in the earlier parliaments. Perhaps the explanation lies in the removal of the hated Mary Stuart, and a growing but unspoken recognition that her son James, raised in the Calvinist faith, would succeed Elizabeth when she died. Peter Wentworth, however, was not satisfied, and in 1593 his intention to air the matter in Parliament was frustrated only by his imprisonment.

The declining concern about such matters, or their disappearance from the parliamentary scene, distinguishes the parliaments of the late 1580s and the 1590s from the earlier Elizabethan assemblies. After the abortive Presbyterian bills of 1584/85 and 1586/87, the activities of earlier promoters of both moderate and radical reform dwindled to the occasional introduction of measures against pluralities (1589 and 1601). In 1593 James Morrice introduced two bills against what he regarded as the use of unlawful oaths and illegal imprisonment by the Court of High Commission [131 *pp. 194–5*]. It was an audacious move, but its purpose was not reform, only defence against the ecclesiastical courts. In the later 1580s, and certainly during the 1590s, war, its cost and consequences, became the central concern of parliaments. In a political climate created by the stresses and burdens of war, and aggravated in the closing years of the century by inflation and poor harvests, the grievances raised in Parliament focused on money, administrative abuses such as purveyance (especially in 1589), and misuse of the prerogative, notably in the grant of harmful monopolies in 1597/98 and 1601 [92; 72, II *pp. 352–6, 376–93*]. Robert Beale, Clerk of the Privy Council, favoured Morrice's stand against ecclesiastical courts in 1593. If, however, as was reported, he spoke in the same Parliament against an increased grant of taxation to the Crown, he was in this, perhaps, more representative of the priorities and concerns of members of the later Elizabethan war parliaments.

RELATIONS BETWEEN THE LORDS AND COMMONS

Co-operation between the two houses was essential to the success of conciliar strategy. If the Lords and Commons publicly disagreed, the Queen would exploit such divisions and it would not be possible to mount the concerted pressure necessary to overcome her resistance. Therefore, as William Cecil was manager of the Council's covert involvement in such lobbying, his elevation to a peerage in February 1571 required an adjustment in his managerial methods. He was no longer personally present to direct official operations in the Commons. The problem was not that, as Neale saw it, the Lords was amenable to royal wishes and presented no managerial problems, whereas the assertive, rising Lower House did (see above, p. 20). It is important to set aside his misconceived view of Parliament and its two houses. The Lords was the institutional equal of the Commons, and enactment of statute required the assent of both houses as well as that of the monarch. Furthermore, in its social and political influence the Lords was much superior. With its clientage network in the Lower House and its intimate involvement in Court, Council and the government of the Church, its conduct was often the key to productive parliaments. When, in the early seventeenth century, Sir Edward Coke analysed the causes of unsuccessful parliaments, he identified five: 'when the king hath been in displeasure with his Lords or with his Commons; when any of the great lords were at variance between themselves'; disputes between the two houses; disorder within the Commons; and inadequate preparation by the Council [4, IV *p. 35*]. The Lords' role loomed large. As Coke sat in the Commons in 1589 and 1593 (when he was Speaker) and attended the Lords in 1597 and 1601, in his capacity as attorney general, his opinions should not be treated lightly. Burghley's managerial problem was not an obstreperous, but an unwieldy, inefficient Lower House (see pp. 79–84).

Furthermore, relations between the two houses were characterised by harmony and co-operation rather than friction. Of course there were exceptions. The Commons was conscious of the Lords' social superiority, and individual knights and burgesses did not question this as part of the natural order of things. However, there was at times, especially in the 1570s and 1580s, a corporate sensitivity and tetchiness in the Commons' dealings with the Upper House. This was rarely expressed on important matters but on points of procedure and protocol. When, in 1581, the Lords returned a Commons' amendment to a bill against sedition, because it had not been endorsed by the Clerk, 'for want whereof their lordships had no warrant to deal therewith any further', the omission was immediately rectified. However, the Commons then counter-attacked on a technicality. It resolved that, as the Lords had further amended some of its own additions and alterations to the bill, without actually rejecting the original changes, it should send up the measure to their lordships and leave it with them 'as a bill that this house cannot deal withal'. The next day the Lords protested that the Lower House had re-drafted one of its bills, without prior consultation and against all precedent, to which the Commons tartly replied, 'that this house had cause to do as they did, and might likewise well do so' [21 *pp. 132–4*]. When, a few days later, the subsidy bill passed the Lords, it was returned to the Commons, as the initiator thereof. However, the accompanying message, that it did not really matter in which House the bill resided until the end of the session, ruffled the Commons' feathers. It expostulated that 'the use thereof is not indifferent, but always hath been and is that it be sent down into this house and not left there' [21 *p. 136*].

It all looks rather childish, but precedent and customary practices were to be respected; and, it should be added, the Lords was not above reproach. Furthermore, the Commons' sensitivity is not surprising, because of the greater social muscle, prestige and relative antiquity of the Upper House. Members were particularly conscious of their inferior status and political disadvantage when delegates of the two houses met in joint conference. Such discussions grew in frequency and importance during the reign, in order to pre- empt time-consuming disagreements, hammer out differences, and save desirable bills from rejection in the other chamber. However, knights and burgesses were at a serious psychological disadvantage when they stood bare-headed whilst the Lords' delegates remained seated and wore their hats, and some of them were intimidated on such occasions. Consequently, the Commons' general recognition of the value of joint conferences was tempered with caution, especially the resolution of 1581, that its delegates should not agree to anything new proposed at a joint conference until the House had given its approval [*Doc. 29*].

There was clearly a concern amongst some MPs that the Upper House used joint conferences as a way of managing them. Indeed, it was the increased incidence of such conferences in the middle parliaments of the reign which resulted in most of the Elizabethan intercameral disagreements: for example, over bills concerning the justices of the forests and apparel (1576), the Scottish borders (1581), a measure on land conveyances which enjoyed the Queen's personal support (1584/85), and a private bill dealing with the sale of Thomas Handford's lands (1586/87) [132 *pp. 213–14*].

Occasionally, a sharp disagreement could develop into a more serious and extended dispute. This, in turn, could result in the loss of the bill under consideration. One such case concerned the heir of Charles, Lord Stourton, who had been executed for murder in the previous reign. Although conviction for felony, unlike treason, did not extinguish the title, it tainted the blood of the culprit's descendants. Elizabeth must have smiled favourably on the heir, John Lord Stourton. She summoned him to Parliament in 1576, when he attained his majority, and she signed a grace bill which would restore him in blood and so enable him to inherit property and defend his rights in the law courts. It passed the Lords smoothly and without demur, but the Commons modified it. When the Upper

House protested at this mishandling of a bill which followed so many precedents and, moreover, had been signed by the Queen and so should pass, the Commons grew angry. It charged its parliamentary partner with threats to its liberties and claimed the right to alter any bill, even one endorsed by Elizabeth. Furthermore, it refused to justify its conduct and dismissed the request for a conference on the grounds that, as it held the bill, it should initiate a joint discussion [21 *pp. 114–15*]. There followed a series of heated exchanges, eventually a joint conference during which the Lords subjected the Commons' delegates to shabby treatment, and the obdurate refusal of the Lower House to alter its stand. Time ran out and the bill failed to pass. Typically, much of the heat engendered in the Commons had nothing to do with Stourton's case. It was caused by the Lords' rejection of a bill which the Commons had passed a few days before, concerning general property rights [72, I *pp. 356–9*].

Such clashes were understandable as both chambers worked towards the resolution of problems and questions pertaining to joint conferences – in particular, who should initiate them and in what circumstances? The Stourton episode clarified one important procedural point, that only the House in possession of a bill should move for a joint meeting about it, regardless of where it began its parliamentary passage. It was the Commons' failure to do so, before replacing a Lords' bill with one of its own, that caused some of the disputes of the 1580s. When they occurred, even Privy Councillors such as Sir Walter Mildmay and Lord Burghley stood with their respective houses and publicly disagreed. Most of these disagreements, however, were simply teething pains, as Lords and Commons slowly proceeded to a formalisation and standardisation of the purpose and procedure of joint conferences. Even during this process, in the middle years of the reign, the Commons sometimes called for conferences and bills dealt with in them often became law. They were, after all, a quick and simple way of ironing out differences and securing the approval of the other House for proposed alterations and additions. This was acknowledged in 1589 by Thomas Snagge, the Commons' Speaker, when he ruled that future joint conferences would be called to solicit the opinion of the House of origin, in order to avoid the possible loss of bills [132 *pp. 211–17*].

Nevertheless, the Commons' caution about joint conferences was justified in 1593, when there occurred the most serious confrontation of the reign. It concerned the lay subsidy, which the Commons alone could initiate. In contrast, the Lords could do no more than affirm or reduce (but not increase) the proposed tax.

However, Elizabeth's government was financially straitened by the demands of war and no one knew that better than her Lord Treasurer. When the Commons, repeating its exceptional grant of 1589, voted two subsidies, the Upper House requested a joint conference, at which its spokesman, Burghley, demanded more, a triple subsidy. There was, in fact, a precedent for the Lords' more active role in determining the size of the grant. In Mary I's last Parliament (1558) a joint conference, called for by the Upper House, had decided on the size of the grant, the subsidy rates and number of instalments [55 *pp. 160–1*; 56 *pp. 407–8*]. Nevertheless, Burghley's demand provoked an angry outburst, furious debate and a protest at the Lords' infringement of the Commons' liberties. Although the Lower House agreed to a further meeting of its delegation with that of the Lords, this was to be a 'general conference', without yielding to Burghley's specific demand. In the end, however, it surrendered with what good grace it could muster and 'gladly and cheerfully' voted the requisite sum. So the Commons retained its sole right to initiate grants of taxation and to determine the amount, whilst the Crown obtained larger supply [72, II *pp. 298–312*; 132]. The subsidy episode of 1593 illustrates not only the authority of Burghley in particular and of the Lords in general, in their relations with the Commons, but also their use of joint conferences in order to manage it.

At the same time such confrontations were the exception and not the norm of Elizabethan parliamentary history. The ramifications of patronage, kinship, friendship, royal service, professional and economic associations, linked many bishops, peers, gentry and burgesses within a relatively close-knit governing class. It was in stark contrast to the division of continental assemblies into competing and often hostile social orders and estates of clergy, nobility and commons. In England that medieval concept of estates had given way to the idea that Crown, Lords and Commons constituted the three parliamentary estates. Social homogeneity certainly smoothed the passage of business within the bicameral Parliament. The links between the membership of the two houses were also significant. Many peers had previous experience of the Commons. Some of the bishops and nobles exercised electoral patronage, and wielded influence over MPs, through the occupancy of county offices and the possession of large estates [58; 132]. The variety of connections helped to ensure that relations between the Lords and Commons were not, any more than Puritanism or Court factions, a cause of serious conflict in Elizabethan parliaments.

7 THE BUSINESS RECORD OF ELIZABETHAN PARLIAMENTS

Elizabethan parliaments had a number of important functions, as points of contact and opportunities for careerist lawyers and ambitious gentlemen to seek recruitment into the Queen's service, but it was not for these reasons that they were summoned. Likewise, they were not a sixteenth-century political version of the Roman hippodrome or gladiatorial arena: obviously they were not called in order to engage in political conflict, competition and opposition to the Crown (see pp. 18, 43). The only reason for their existence was the Crown's need for money, laws and sometimes counsel (for example, on religion or national security). Whichever of these was Elizabeth's priority on any given occasion, the parliamentary end-product was a statute. In other words, the prime function of parliaments, indeed their very *raison d'être,* was legislation. The fact that criticism and disagreement occurred during the law-making process is hardly surprising. Even a Crown and governing class which were in essential harmony and believed in consensus politics could not always achieve general agreement. There were, in any case, issues such as the succession, religion and misuse of royal authority which could divide members and Councillors against each other and amongst themselves.

THE PURPOSE OF PARLIAMENTS: RECORDS AND PROCEDURES

The chief function of parliaments, that of legislation [94 *pp. 99–102*], determined the shape and content of their records. So the journals kept by the Clerks of the two houses were above all records of business designed to assist them in their work, in particular the readings, engrossment and commitment of bills [66 *pp. 6–9*]. Additional matter – privilege cases, especially in the Commons (see pp. 44–6, 109–13), the record of proxies and the attendance register for the Lords (see pp. 35, 106) – also had a utilitarian purpose. One thing is quite clear. The survival of a Commons' journal from 1547 and its evolution thereafter are not, as Neale claimed [85 *pp. 136–70*; 65 *p. 82*], signs of the political maturation or rise of the Lower House. The Underclerks had been compiling such records long before then [65 *pp. 84–5*]. Furthermore, variations in the form and content of the Elizabethan Commons' journal were simply due to the different practices of particular Clerks, the accidents of survival (whether a scribbled original or a fair copy) and the managerial needs of Lord Burghley who required information on proceedings there [26 *pp. 262–7*]. Other parliamentary records, too, are institutional rather than political detritus. Surviving paper bills, the original parchment Acts, the text of public Acts written on to the Parliament Roll by the Lords' Clerk after the session, and the Queen's printer's edition of statutes (circulated throughout the country for the information of magistrates who had to enforce them) were all products of the legislative process [66 *pp. 4–6*; 75; 77].

Similarly, procedural developments were signs of institutional improvement, not of political growth [26 *pp. 267–8*]. The fact that most innovations and refinements in procedure occurred in the Commons is a commentary on its more primitive state earlier in the century. In contrast, the early Tudor Lords was an older chamber with recognised and well-proved procedures, even if they were flexibly applied. However, in Elizabeth's reign this flexibility gradually gave way to a more rigid practice and bureaucratic routine. The procedural evolution was stimulated by a process of cross-fertilisation. The Commons adopted practices long-tested in the Lords, whilst, at the same time, it too was innovating. Because a number of its members were ennobled, some of its novelties were transmitted with them to the Upper House. Most of these changes related to the essential legislative purpose of parliaments. Gradually, the two houses moved towards the three-reading procedure as the most practical way to make law. It took into account contemporary realities; in particular, it was designed to meet the needs of legislators who did not have access to printed copies of bills presented for their consideration. Therefore, the first reading was a literal reading of the text and its purpose was to inform members of its contents. The next stage was a notional second reading, the real purpose of which was to debate the substance of the bill. If necessary, it was then referred to a bill committee for revision, or even re-drafting. Once the committee had completed its work and secured the Commons' approval of its amendments, the original paper bill was engrossed – that is, written out on parchment. This again was a sensible practice because, by then, a bill might be disfigured by deletions and interlineations and needed to be written in fair copy. Furthermore, once it had passed the major hurdle of a second reading in the House of origin, the chances of its eventual passage into law were greatly enhanced. Therefore it needed to be recorded on parchment, which was more durable than paper. Finally, there was a third reading confined to textual precision. Only then was the fate of a bill decided, by acclamation or a division in the Commons and by the Clerk's head-count in the Lords as each bishop and peer said 'content' or 'not content'. Because the assent of both houses was necessary, the three-reading procedure was repeated in the second chamber (except for the engrossment, of course). If a bill negotiated that stage successfully, it then awaited the royal assent at the end of the session. That was not a formality. Elizabeth vetoed seventy-two bills during her reign.

This is in an idealised description of parliamentary practice. As the two houses moved towards a standardised three-reading procedure, there were still many variations, aberrations and anomalies. Bills might have more or less than three readings or no committee stage. Sometimes this was simply due to defective recording by the Clerks, but in other instances it indicated a flexible, easy-going application of the procedure which was slow to disappear. It was not uncommon either for one House to redraft or propose amendments to a bill which had already passed the other. The picture of procedural development is not a neat and tidy one. Nevertheless, there was an inexorable movement towards uniformity and a gradual elimination of anomalies, and the records of the parliamentary bureaucrats reflect this trend. If a bill had, for example, four or five readings, Tudor Clerks modified the numbering in order to adhere to the accepted norm of three. They anticipated procedural uniformity but, at the same time, they reinforced the movement towards it.

Innovations in legislative practice must be seen in this institutional context, and not misread as political devices which were designed to free parliamentary proceedings from conciliar control. The classic example is the late Elizabethan–early Stuart development of the general committee, later styled the Committee of the Whole House. When the Commons went into Committee of the Whole House it replaced the Speaker, notoriously a royal nominee, with an elected chairman. Formal rules of debate were set aside and members could speak as often as they might on the bill before them. Notestein grasped the procedural niceties of general committees well enough, but he misunderstood their purpose and significance. He argued that, if they were not an opposition design to rid the House of official control, they were at least a convenience which achieved the same result [73 *pp. 37–8*]. In fact, the innovation was nothing of the kind. It was not politically motivated, but a device to improve efficiency and speed up business by dispensing with the formalities and restrictions of set debate. Furthermore, the inspiration behind it derived, not from a parliamentary opposition, but from the Privy Council.

In the same way, the appointment of Privy Councillors to Commons' bill committees was not determined by a specific political motive, the maintenance of political control. At no time in Elizabeth's reign did her Council exercise control. Nor could a handful of men, diminishing in number later in the reign, have done so, although they could exercise some influence and provide a degree of guidance, especially with the assistance of a support network of clients and loyalists (see pp. 85–9). R.C. Munden's analysis of Commons' committees reveals that Councillors were most consistently appointed to those dealing with 'commonwealth grievances', such as monopolies and purveyance, and bills to do with 'royal policies and finance'. He concludes that they were appointed by the procedure of a 'formula' appointment, like any other interest group, to committees in which they had a particular interest – in their case the royal interest [84].

THE PRIVY COUNCIL AND REQUESTS FOR SUPPLY

It was for long generally accepted by historians that parliamentary taxation was traditionally sought and granted only for extraordinary, usually military needs, especially actual or pending war. This, however, has been challenged in recent years. G.R. Elton, for example, presented a case for significant innovation in its purpose. In 1534 and 1553 royal government successfully sought grants in peace-time, on the grounds that it needed parliamentary assistance to meet its ordinary expenses. The preamble of each of the subsidy Acts of 1534 and 1553 emphasised, as a justification for a peace-time tax, the nation's gratitude for the blessings of the monarch's fruitful and caring governance. According to Elton Elizabeth I, building on this foundation, especially the general acceptance that peace-time taxation was now necessary, regularly secured parliamentary grants which were given, not to conduct war, but because she had preserved the peace [44]. There was much to commend this argument: not only the preambles to the subsidy Acts, but also the lack of evidence of a tight-fisted or antagonistic Commons' attitude, when confronted with royal requests for supply at times when England was not at war. This thesis – that there occurred in the sixteenth century an important innovation in both the justification and the occasions of parliamentary taxation – was itself innovatory. It was questioned and criticised, but it also received significant support [108; 109; 122 *pp. 1174–5*]. J.D. Alsop argued not only that subsidies and fifteenths and tenths – extraordinary revenue – were used to defray ordinary expenses in the years of 'peace', but also that parliaments did not cavil, obstruct or resist such royal revenue requests [108 *pp. 5–17, 27–8*; 109 *pp. 91–4*]. Recently, however, R.W. Hoyle has challenged the 'revisionist' position of Elton and Alsop that the old and clear distinction between ordinary Crown revenue and extraordinary revenue from taxation broke down and that, from the 1530s, Parliament willingly provided money for ordinary government expenses. Instead, Hoyle has reasserted the older view that war and parliamentary taxation continued to be closely related [122].

There is something to be said for both positions. The Queen requested and received grants from all but one (1572) of the parliaments which met before England drifted into undeclared war with Spain. It is inaccurate, however, to label these as 'peace' parliaments, as if the government was not involved in military adventures and actions before it despatched an expedition to the Low Countries in 1585/86. English interventions to help the Scottish Protestants (1560) and French Huguenots (1562–63), operations against Shane O'Neill in Ireland (1561–67) and the suppression of the northern earls' rebellion in England (1569) did not amount to full-scale war, but they all cost money. In each case Elizabeth's government sought retrospective parliamentary assistance in order to meet what were extraordinary charges [*Doc. 30*]. To this extent at least there was no radical change in Elizabethan attitudes to the purpose of the subsidy. Furthermore, when Privy Councillors in the Commons set forth the reasons why the Queen needed money, they often referred specifically to defensive requirements, such as 'the provision of armour and the navy' (1563) or, in 1571, 'the preparation and setting forth of ships for the defence against all foreign forces, suspected and intended' [108]. They, and the preambles of subsidy Acts (as in 1566), made reference to 'great *extraordinary* charges sustained in the defence of your majesty's dominions' (my emphasis). Nevertheless, as national security and defence were amongst the chief ongoing responsibilities of the monarchs, so they were to be accounted amongst the *ordinary* expenses of government [*Doc. 30*]. Furthermore, as noted above, the subsidy preambles also justified supply as a reward for the quality of Elizabeth's governance [66 *pp. 154–5*]. Hoyle, however, counters this with the argument that the function of the preamble had changed. To a great extent it had lost its informative or 'educative' purpose and become, rather, a eulogistic piece about the Queen [122 *pp. 1191–6*].

Such differences of interpretation have not been resolved, but one thing is clear. Although Elizabeth's Privy Councillors sometimes had other and hidden agendas, she called parliaments chiefly for money. Furthermore, it was her Council's responsibility to obtain it. As the years passed by, Councillors became more efficient in their preparations and more effective in their control of taxation proceedings in the Commons. In some of the earlier parliaments, 1563 and 1571 for example, the subject of supply was first raised by a private member, doubtless by prearrangement with Councillors [21 *p. 63*; 10 *p. 202*]. Thereafter, the introduction of the topic, and the justification and motion for supply, were the responsibility of the Chancellor of the Exchequer (Sir Walter Mildmay in 1576–88/89, and Sir John Fortescue in 1597) or Sir Robert Cecil in 1593 and 1601 [10 *pp. 440–4, 502–8*; 72, II *pp. 54–6, 168, 204–5, 298, 358–9, 411*]. Although the constitutional theory was that the Commons alone could initiate lay taxation, that theory differed markedly from practice. An experienced member advised a Privy Councillor in 1572 that one way to despatch business more quickly was to have 'the subsidy book ready written both in paper and parchment' [1 *fol. 35*]. In other words, the Council should draw up not only the proposed terms of the tax, but also the final draft of the bill, before the session began. Then, in 1581, Thomas Norton, Burghley's client, pre-empted the Commons' role. He collaborated with Chancellor Mildmay, dominated the huge committee named to consider the subsidy and the bill against Catholic recusants, and drew the 'articles and heads' of the two measures. Moreover, he probably produced the final drafts as well [96 *pp. 31–2*].

The purpose of such managerial practices was the efficient (and preferably rapid) passage of the subsidy bill. They were not prompted by the expectation of resistance to requests for supply, nor by the experience of Commons' opposition in previous parliaments. There is no positive evidence that even peace-time taxation caused parliamentary opposition. Indeed, the only serious trouble occurred when, in 1593, the House of Lords appeared to pre-empt the Commons' right to initiate supply. The Lower House was consistently receptive and responsive to the Queen's financial needs. Nor, at any time in the reign, did it attempt to take political advantage of its initiating role by making a tax grant conditional upon prior redress of grievances. According to Neale, in 1566 some members of the Commons engaged in an organised attempt to link the subsidy bill with a suit to the Queen to settle the succession. This, however, has been disproved. Blackmail of such a kind was not a feature of the Elizabethan parliamentary landscape [72, I *p. 139*; 89 *pp. 223–6*]. On the other hand, although the Queen disliked long sessions, time was allowed for the enactment of private and personal measures after the passage of the subsidy [65 *p. 93*]. Nevertheless, members, who were sensitive about the expectations of their electorates and aware of her desire for a speedy conclusion, were anxious to push through the bills entrusted to them. In 1601 Robert Wingfield 'moved the house that, seeing the subsidy was granted and they yet had done nothing, it would please her majesty not to dissolve the parliament until some acts were passed' [20 *p. 204*].

THE LOCALITIES AND THE QUEST FOR BENEFICIAL LAWS

This highlights the Council's ongoing managerial problem. Since the 1530s the novel omnicompetence and sovereignty of statute had made Parliament increasingly popular as a clearing-house of legislative business. The volume of local, sectional and personal bills steadily grew, accompanied by a refinement of the arts of politicking and lobbying. Inevitably, London took the lead, if only because it could utilise its great wealth, civic organisation, proximity to Whitehall, Court and Council contacts, and the seats which its four members occupied next to the Privy Councillors in the Commons. Furthermore, its diverse and geographically wide-ranging economic activities could be advanced through parliaments and, at the same time, protected from rival urban communities which, like Yarmouth and other outports, felt themselves under threat from the City's economic expansionism. The London lobby was the most sophisticated in the Elizabethan parliaments, drafting bills and making provision for payments to those willing to support them, in particular to parliamentary officials. Thus the Commons' Clerk frequently received a gratuity of forty shillings. The Speaker enjoyed more generous treatment. His customary gift of £6 13s 4d had doubled by the end of the reign. Elizabethan gratuities were not necessarily bribes, but when, in 1593 and 1597, the Court of Aldermen of the City of London sent a deputation to the Speaker's lodgings to seek his 'favour' for certain of their bills, their accompanying gifts deserve no other description. Aldermen were prepared to lobby Burghley and other Councillors and to canvass the Lords in order to advance their own measures and obstruct others which might harm the City's interests [71 *pp. 337–8, 384, 387; 26 pp. 261–2*].

Other cities and towns were engaged in similar practices at a more modest level. Westminster tipped the Commons' Clerk, and in 1572 Worcester purchased two cheeses for the Speaker in its unsuccessful attempt to secure the passage of a bill concerning the River Severn. York's assembly regularly issued instructions to its representatives to advance its bills and, in particular, to secure exemption from parliamentary taxes. Exeter, too, despatched its members with local measures, money to lay out in their promotion and, in 1601, with orders to consult Sir Robert Cecil, the city's High Steward, about its interests [79 *pp. 146, 280, 292–5*; 116 *pp. 154–5*]. Frequently, towns and rival economic lobbies within urban centres were in conflict as they promoted bills and tried to defeat measures promoted by others: Bristol against Gloucester; Yarmouth against Lowestoft; and, in London, brewers in conflict with the Coopers' Company and the City government, armourers with blacksmiths, and curriers with cordwainers [93; 114; 115; 116]. A crisis in the English fishing industry, caused by successful Dutch competitors, also engendered a particularly lengthy parliamentary quarrel between rival interests: on the one hand, the London Fishmongers' Company, who were buying fish cheaply from the Dutch, and on the other the herring fishermen led by Yarmouth. In 1581 a statute, the terms of which were beneficial to English fishermen and harmful to importers of fish, was enacted by Parliament. After a long campaign the Fishmongers' Company secured modifications of this Act in 1597 and 1601 [95].

In recent studies David Dean, Ian Archer and Robert Tittler have demonstrated how localities, both counties and boroughs (including unenfranchised towns such as Lowestoft), and economic interests formed active lobbies and became well-versed in the arts of parliamentary politicking [93; 110; 116; 117; 118 *pp. 82–92*; 127] [*Doc. 31*]. The willingness of boroughs and other local and sectional interests to use parliaments for their own purposes resulted in a spate of private bills. These dealt with a wide range of local concerns, such as the statutory security of endowments and property ownership, municipal power to raise money by local levies for public works, and a range of beneficial Acts for ports, harbours and havens and particular local economic interests [116 *pp. 146–52*]. Members of the Commons were not concerned only to advance local and sectional causes. On occasions they also sought to promote personal interests, whilst localities were sometimes active in wider commonweal matters, such as poor relief and the protection of English trade and fisheries. However, it was not these but bills in the interest of corporations, economic lobbies, towns and other localities, which constituted the bulk of the private members' legislative input. Most of them began in the Commons, where the knights and burgesses were concerned and often obliged to promote parochial, petty and personal measures for the communities which had returned them. However, for reasons of tactics and timing, it was not unknown for their bills to be entered into the Lords first [*Doc. 31*]. Furthermore, both lords spiritual and temporal were willing to hand in personal and private measures, for themselves or on behalf of their kin and localities.

Nevertheless, it was the Commons which shouldered the main burden of legislative business: eighty-two out of ninety-eight bills before Parliament began there in 1559; ninety-eight of the 131 in 1563; 278 of the 355 (or 78 per cent) during the three sessions of the Parliament of 1572–81. In the later Elizabethan parliaments (1584–1601) the proportions did not significantly alter: 79 per cent of all Acts and failed bills originated in the Lower House. What did this mean in practical terms? In 1572, for example, the Commons had thirty-nine working sessions – altogether about 120–150 hours. The campaign to secure the execution of Norfolk and the attainder of Mary Stuart occupied much time during twenty-one of these sessions. The House also considered seventy bills, the first and literal readings of which must have consumed more precious hours. No wonder that so many of them expired through lack of time and only eleven became law. Elizabeth, her Lord Keeper and Burghley repeatedly admonished the Commons to give priority to urgent and public matters rather than private and parochial bills [*Doc. 35*]. Their concern was understandable, because local bills amounted to one-third of all bills in some sessions [116 *p. 146*]. In her last Parliament, in 1601, the Queen was intoning the same message when she instructed the Speaker, through her Lord Keeper, 'to have a special eye and regard not to make new and idle laws and trouble the house with them' but instead 'take in hand matters of greatest moment and consequence' [7 *p. 602*].

The fact that towns, ports, corporations and economic interests ignored such admonitions signified the importance of Parliament as a 'point of contact' between the centre and the localities [23]. There were, however, serious limitations on its usefulness to those seeking legislative solutions to local problems. It was not in permanent existence and for most of the time it was not available. The process of enacting a private bill into law was time-consuming, expensive (especially in fees), and sometimes burdensome to MPs. Failures were frequent and success often came years later at the second or third attempt. Private bills had to compete with each other and with public measures, which were usually accorded priority in what often amounted to a legislative log-jam. A bill might be opposed by conflicting interests: so in 1571, 1581, 1584–85, and 1597–98 the Blacksmiths' Company resisted the armourers' bills, the brewers successfully opposed the coopers' bills in 1593, whilst curriers and cordwainers frequently attempted to overthrow each other's measures. Even if a measure negotiated its way through both houses, its opponents might persuade the Queen to exercise the royal veto [110 *pp. 35–8*; 114; 115; 116 *pp. 143–5, 162*; 127 *pp. 276–8*]. Often the only results of considerable effort and financial outlay were frustration and failure.

It is important, therefore, not to exaggerate the role or importance of Parliament as a solution to local or sectional problems, interests and ambitions. Only one-tenth or less of English towns sought beneficial results through legislation, partly because Parliament was only one amongst a number of ways to achieve them and partly because of its limited usefulness. Permanent institutions, such as the common-law courts of Common Pleas and Exchequer, Chancery, Star Chamber, the Duchy of Lancaster, and especially the Privy Council were more accessible and used more frequently. Localities also utilised personal contacts: the Vintners' Company turned to the Earl of Leicester in the 1560s; Boston enlisted the help of its patrons, Edward Earl of Lincoln and William Cecil; and, in their dispute, Yarmouth and Lowestoft resorted to Privy Councillors and other personal contacts at Court and in the Queen's household. The solutions sought by localities were often prerogative: proclamations, monopolies, charters, licences, conciliar orders or commissions. If, however, Parliament was summoned during the course of unresolved conflict or at a time of unsolved problems, legislation then became an alternative solution [93 *p. 64*; 110 *pp. 18, 38–43*; 114; 115; 116; 127].

PARLIAMENT'S UTILITY IN QUESTION

The Queen's stricture in 1601 (see above, p. 74) was significant, because it illustrated the growing official disapproval of the large number of statutes enacted by each Parliament. In the early Elizabethan assemblies Lord Keeper Bacon's opening address had been concerned with the 'want of laws which needeth to be provided for'. By 1571, however, he was stressing the possible 'superfluity' of laws and questioning whether some might be unnecessarily sharp and burdensome to subjects. Successive Lord Keepers reiterated this point. In 1593 Sir John Puckering went further when he advised that Parliament was not summoned to make new statutes, of which there were already too many, and recommended instead a reduction in the number of existing laws. In 1597 and 1601 his successor, Sir Thomas Egerton, was even more forceful when he called for Parliament 'to prune and cut off' the many existing laws which were obsolete, obscure, burdensome, too punitive, or loose and slack.

By then Egerton's voice was but one in a swelling chorus of concern: Sir Edward Coke, as Commons' Speaker in 1593, other practising lawyers such as Francis Bacon, Serjeant Harris and William Wiseman, and informed members like Sir Edward Hoby. Committees were named to reduce the excessive number of penal laws, in particular in 1584–85, 1597 and 1601 [20 *pp. 60, 80, 102–3, 178, 180–1; 7 pp. 60, 137, 193, 458–9, 599*]. The House also adopted Bacon's resolution of 1601 that, as there was in each Parliament a committee to renew Acts with a limited life, so there should be one for the repeal of superfluous statutes. A committee was duly appointed and it bore fruit in an Act to continue some laws and annul others [20 *p. 194*]. This was all very commendable, but one must question the sincerity of some of these would-be reformers. Francis Bacon prefaced his introduction of a new bill of weights and measures in 1601 with the artful comment that 'because I would observe the advice that was given in the beginning of this parliament, that we should make no new laws, I have made this bill only a confirmation of the statute of II Henry 7 with a few additions' [20 *p. 190*]. Nevertheless, there was a growing volume of publicly stated opinion that laws needed to be simplified and reduced, and that codification and effective enforcement of those which existed were more beneficial than making new ones. On the other hand, it did not signify that the government had lost interest in Parliament's legislative functions. To assume that would be to misread the way in which it operated. What are often described as policies were usually *ad hoc* responses to situations as they occurred. Certainly, each Tudor monarch had a foreign policy, but this was a prerogative matter and the legislative involvement of parliaments was confined to the voting of war revenue. So far as internal affairs were concerned, probably only one chief Tudor minister, Thomas Cromwell, had some kind of co-ordinated policy. However, he was operating in a period of acute crisis, even though his vision of the way in which state and society should be structured transcended the immediate needs imposed by that crisis. Only in religious matters did successive post-Cromwellian regimes, under Edward VI, Mary, and in Elizabeth's first year, have positive programmes which they had to implement through parliaments.

Thereafter the conservative partnership of Queen and minister sought to preserve the *status quo*, Elizabeth in the Church and William Cecil with his old-fashioned approach to economic and social problems. This was illustrated by the official initiative behind the sumptuary laws which were designed to regulate apparel in accordance with social rank [66 *pp. 271–3*]. Parliaments were not steps in the unfolding of some grand design, as perhaps they had been in the 1530s or in 1553–55, albeit even then things had not always gone according to plan. Instead, they became part of the normal *ad hoc* nature of government. They were called to fund Elizabethan government or respond to specific political crises: the northern rebellion and papal excommunication (1569–70), Mary Stuart (1572 and 1586–87), and the coming of the seminary priests and Jesuit mission (1581). Sometimes Councillors had an ulterior motive when they persuaded the Queen to summon yet another assembly (see pp. 56–9). However, usually they, too, were reacting to a particular event. So, for example, their stage-management of the succession campaign of 1563 was a response to Elizabeth's near-fatal bout of smallpox in the previous year. Naturally, Councillors used the occasion of a Parliament to enact new laws which they considered, at that moment, to be necessary for good government. But this was a haphazard affair and it did not amount to an organised, coherent legislative programme. This was as true of the 1560s as it was of the 1590s. There were, for example, few great legislative monuments to official economic and social planning. One notable exception was the famous Act of Artificers (Apprentices) in 1563. According to S.T. Bindoff it was primarily the product of the Commons' herculean labours [111]. Elton's reconstruction of its passage, however, has shown it to be a conciliar initiative, combining two official bills of 1559, along with additions made during its enactment in 1563 [66 *pp. 263–7*]. Another long-term commonweal concern of the government was the related problems of poverty, unemployment and vagabondage. The poor law of 1572, which introduced a compulsory poor rate, was official, but it derived from a private initiative of the previous year's Parliament. Another conciliar measure to provide work for the poor was enacted in 1576. And in 1597 and 1601 the codified Poor Relief Acts were passed. Impressive as they were, they must also be seen as immediate palliatives in the current economic crisis of the 1590s. Furthermore, in their final form and scope they owed much to parliamentary input as well as to conciliar initiative.

The simple fact is that the Elizabethan Council did not gradually lose interest in the legislative function of parliaments. After 1559 it regularly took the initiative when it required a subsidy, it was faced with political or economic crises, or it deemed more laws to be necessary for effective government. In addition, Councillors actively supported other measures. When in 1563 William Cecil approved of a bill to strengthen the merchant navy, he added a clause making Wednesday a compulsory fish day – known thereafter as 'Cecil's fast' – and steered the measure through the Commons [72, I *pp. 114–16*]. However, the bill had been drafted by a Commons' committee, not by the Council. Only in a loose sense can it be called an official bill, because it originated in a motion by Elizabeth's admiral, William Winter, and her chief adviser backed it [21 *p. 65*; 79, I *p. 676*]. Furthermore, the principle of cabinet unanimity did not exist, the Council was often divided, and Councillors who lent support to particular measures did not always have the co-operation of colleagues. Once again, the 1590s differed little from the 1560s. The growing official disapproval of more new laws in the later Elizabethan parliaments was probably an expression of hard-headed political realism. Their enactment used up parliamentary time which could be better spent on official business. In any case, the Queen and her advisers were better qualified to view new laws in the broader perspective of their enforcement. Statutes were made easily enough, but could they be implemented? This sensible attitude, however, did not reduce significantly either the legislative output or conciliar initiative when new laws were considered necessary. The sessions of 1559–81 averaged thirty-five Acts and those of 1584–1601 thirty. Furthermore, if the 1586–87 Parliament, with its central concern of Mary Stuart and a mere ten Acts, is excluded, the average for the later period rises to thirty-four.

In contrast, Elizabethan parliaments did not fulfil their financial function, especially during the long war with Spain. The fifteenth and tenth (a tax on rural and urban movables) had ossified into a system of compositions (or fixed levies on each county) and sixteenth-century inflation seriously eroded their real value. Cardinal Wolsey's experiment with the subsidy, an income tax, at first boosted the Crown's parliamentary revenue. However, after Henry VIII's reign the efficiency of assessment and collection declined and so did the yield. Wealthier Elizabethans were scandalously under-rated. The peers' average assessed annual income steadily declined from £750 to £311, and this despite inflation [124 *p. 18*]. Sir Walter Raleigh spoke the truth in 1601 when he told fellow gentlemen in the Commons that their estates, rated at £30 or £40 in the subsidy books, were 'not the hundredth part of our wealth' [20 *p. 204*]. Some evaded taxation altogether. Admittedly, the House made a compensatory gesture by voting two subsidies in 1589, three in 1593 and four in 1601, but until 1593 these were paid only in annual instalments of half a subsidy. This was pathetically inadequate during the war with Spain. It was less the fault of parliaments than of the general reluctance to pay what amounted to annual taxation, especially during the lengthy economic recession in the 1590s. Nevertheless, parliaments were not adequately funding a financially straitened government. However, Elizabeth and Burghley did not energetically exploit hereditary revenues (like feudal dues) or systematically explore other possible extra-parliamentary sources, such as impositions (additional customs duties) or ship money. Instead, they repeatedly turned to parliaments to finance the war and combat the state's growing indebtedness. That is why Burghley demanded a triple subsidy in 1593 (see pp. 64–5). Queen and minister contemplated no alternative.

THE COMMONS' INEFFICIENCY

As Parliament rendered vital services to Elizabethan government, it was of continuing concern to the Privy Council that one of its houses, the Commons, was so inefficient. It was large, unwieldy and growing larger (see pp. 12, 30–1). Size was not an inherent disadvantage, but it could be when so many members were inexperienced. T.E. Hartley has calculated that two-thirds of Elizabethan members sat in only one Parliament [68 *pp. 105–7*]. Usually about half its members were novices [71 *p. 309*], ignorant of procedures or how to conduct themselves in committee or debate. William Fleetwood highlighted the problem in his report to his patron, Lord Burghley, during the opening days in 1584. He described the knights and burgesses 'out of all order, in troops standing upon the floor making strange noises, there being not past seven or eight of the old parliament'. Then, when Councillors made the customary motion for election of the Speaker of their choice, in this case Sir John Puckering, the House remained silent. This was a token of ignorance, not hostility. Members did not know what to do next. Fleetwood did, whispering to those about him, 'Cry Puckering'. Then, 'they and I beginning, the rest did the same'. His account of a bill committee likewise illustrates the confusion which could characterise Commons' proceedings – worsened by the rule that any member could attend and speak at a committee. Obviously, lots of curious novices did so, because sixty or more turned up at the afternoon meeting, even though the committee numbered only thirty-three. The old Parliament man contemptuously dismissed them as 'all young gents' of whom 'twenty at once did speak. And there we sat talking and did nothing until night, so that Mr Chancellor was weary. And then we departed home' [9 *fol. 45*].

The Council did what it could to resolve the problem. When Elizabeth summoned a Parliament in 1586 to consider Mary Stuart's fate, the Council circularised sheriffs, recommending the re-election of those who had sat in 1584. Men of experience were needed to handle this urgent and weighty cause, especially those who, in the previous Parliament, had passed the Act for the Queen's Safety, under the terms of which Mary was to be tried. In elections the Council's wishes were respected in only 52 per cent of the seats; this must have been disappointing, even when allowance is made for natural wastage from death, age and illness [79, I *p. 39*]. It was a commentary on the autonomy of the electoral system, which was more susceptible to the workings of contemporary social mechanisms, such as the patron–client relationship, than to official intervention. The House continued to be plagued with novices, carpet-baggers, some of whom were ignorant of their parliamentary boroughs' needs, and men who secured election for private, frivolous or selfish reasons (see pp. 31, 44–5, 103–4).

The lack of motivation, interest, experience or ability of many members explains some of the Council's other managerial problems. Proceedings could be noisy and disorderly. Unpopular speeches were subjected to loud chatter, 'hemming', laughing, coughing, hawking and even spitting [7 *pp. 335, 633*]. The Speaker had frequent cause to admonish such interruptions and also sharp and bitter speeches.

Sometimes he had difficulty in restoring order when several members leapt to their feet to speak next and none would give way to the others. Sir Thomas Smith's description of a well-mannered, decorous assembly did not always fit the facts [*Doc. 32*]. Sir Robert Cecil's comment in 1601, when he described the Commons' behaviour as more fit for a grammar school than a court of Parliament, was tactless but also justified [7 *pp. 282, 434, 493–4, 651*]. Garrulous members, too, impaired efficiency, especially as their audience was usually sympathetic or at least tolerant, so long as they did not utter disloyal words or offend the dignity and privileges of the House. After all, this was an age of the spoken word. Lengthy sermons were the vehicle for transmission of the Protestant truth; rhetoric (the art of public speaking) was taught at the universities; and the legal education at the inns of court was based on oral exercises. The ornate orations of Lord Keeper and Speaker at the opening and closing ceremonies of parliaments and the literal first reading of bills fed, but seldom satisfied, the appetites of members. Even ardent loyalists, whose concern was to promote and push through Council business, could obstruct it by their excessive speech. William Fleetwood, for example, was guilty of learned, often amusing, but also long and irrelevant addresses.

These problems not only retarded business, but also contributed to absenteeism. So did the technical and tedious nature of much of Parliament's business which, in the case of local bills, was also of no interest to many members. It might have mattered less if the lawyers, the men best-equipped to draft and amend legislation, had not been so willing to desert the Commons for the more profitable law courts (see pp. 36–7, 107). To some extent this may have been counterbalanced by the election of gentlemen with some knowledge and training in the law (see p. 37). Nevertheless, the circumstances were unfavourable and the Privy Council had to achieve its objectives against the competing claims of time-consuming and often contentious private bills. A few examples will illustrate the problem. The bill to bring the River Lea to London, introduced in 1571, was to all appearances an innocuous, even beneficial measure. Its purpose was to authorise the digging of a canal from the Lea, which flowed south from Hertfordshire, to join the Thames east of the City. This would facilitate grain shipments and benefit both the producers and the voracious metropolis by shortening the journey, by-passing the many mills and meandering course of the lower reaches of the Lea, and avoiding the adverse tides of both the Thames and its tributary. However, the original bill empowered

London to acquire the necessary land and hold it forever on payment of rents at current market values. Furthermore, it probably allowed the City to levy tolls on canal users. Although the bill quickly passed the Lords, it ran into trouble in the Commons, where the proposed rent freeze (and perhaps the tolls) came under fire. Millowners, landowners along the proposed canal route, carters who carried grain to the City, and 'badgers' (the middlemen who bought and sold grain) all feared competition and threats to their livelihoods [120 *pp. 218–23*]. They marshalled their parliamentary forces in the Commons, where the bill was referred to a committee after its first reading – in itself an unusual step by then. Robert Wroth, whose family owned the largest mill on the Lea and many of whose tenants were carters carrying grain to London, was a member of the committee. Later he was involved in local riots of protest against navigational improvements on the river, and as a JP he fined a number of bargemen [120 *p. 223*]. Doubtless he led the lobby which persuaded the bill committee to prohibit tolls and require London to purchase outright the necessary land. Such changes made the canal project more expensive and it was not implemented, although some navigational improvements were carried out [121]. As so often happened, a private bill benefiting one interest threatened others and so bred conflict.

The second example foreshadowed a later project when, in 1614, James I approved the proposal of a London merchant, Sir William Cockayne, that the dyeing and finishing of cloth should be carried out in England, not Flanders. It was a disastrous experiment, which resulted in soaring unemployment and stockpiles of unsold cloth. In 1572 a bill to permit the export of dyed cloth was debated at length. John Marshe, member for London, led the attack against it and secured its rejection [6 *fols 63v–64*]. Thirdly, there were the measures to preserve timber and suppress iron mills. These were intimately related because charcoal was used for iron-smelting. Furthermore, the proliferation of iron mills around London and the consequent depredation of forests threatened the City's cheap fuel supplies. It is not surprising that its members, especially Fleetwood, Marshe, Norton and Sir Rowland Hayward, promoted such bills in 1563, 1571, 1572 and 1576, and dressed up their parochial interests in arguments about the public interest [*Doc. 33*]. Eventually, in 1581 they succeeded, despite Sir Henry Sidney, the powerful spokesman of the iron interest; but it was only a temporary victory, and the parliamentary struggle continued. Other local and sectional measures of an economic nature provoked dispute and frequently failed, the commonest being those concerned with England's staple industry, cloth. Private bills, such as those dealing with Bristol merchants in 1571 [10 *p. 247*], the Earl of Kent's property in 1572 [133 *p. 27*], Sir Richard Wenman's will in 1576 [26 *p. 260*], and the late Sir Thomas Gresham's debts in 1581 [21 *pp. 127–8, 132–3*], could run to many readings and involve arbitration with concerned parties and legal counsel at the bar of the House or before the bill committee.

London frequently promoted or opposed economic measures. Although its success rate was not high, despite intensive lobbying, this did not discourage it. Some bills were devised and promoted by the Mayor and Aldermen. However, London's complex economic structure, which contained many diverse and competing interests, caused individual companies as well to seek a parliamentary solution to their problems: in particular to exclude interlopers, preserve local monopolies, and restrain the harmful activities of other City companies. They were just as willing as the Mayor and Aldermen to politick in the Commons and canvass the Speaker with *douceurs*. London's governors endeavoured to control and diminish the volume of bills. In 1566 the Lord Mayor appointed a special court to scrutinise legislative proposals. It approved some, vetoed others and referred a number for an extra-parliamentary solution. In 1566–67, for example, it ordered the drafting of two bills, approved four for the artificers and vintners and rejected one for the brewers; and in 1572 it vetoed another measure for the artificers and promised to see 'good order therein taken to their quietness'. Nevertheless, despite a further tightening up of procedures later in the reign, companies still circumvented official controls and smuggled their bills into Parliament [5, Rep. 16 *fols 118v–119, 128–128v, 134, 139v–141, 262–262v, 275v, 277*; Rep. 17 *fols. 129v–130, 134v, 141v, 144, 152v, 311v, 335, 337, 343v*; Rep. 18 *fol 130*; Rep. 19 *fols 35, 43, 45v*].

The City government's position was an ambivalent one. It continued to draft measures and instruct its members to promote them, along with those of the companies which it had endorsed. In 1597 it even appointed a legislative committee to devise bills, in a more systematic attempt to promote London's interests [71 *p. 386*]. Its parliamentary representatives also received instructions to obstruct or defeat harmful measures before the Commons [71 *pp. 384–7*]. Amongst the advices received by a Privy Councillor in 1572 were recommendations for dealing with the formidable volume of private bills, especially those of London [*Doc. 34*]. They constitute the best contemporary commentary on the Elizabethan Commons' mediocre performance. Its poor showing is borne out by hard facts. The loss of the later Elizabethan Commons' journals and Sir Simonds D'Ewes's deficiencies [7; 112; see p. 96] make it impossible to calculate precisely the number of bills before the later Elizabethan parliaments. However, the Acts can be totted up, whilst the work of David Dean permits a reasonably accurate assessment of abortive (unsuccessful) bills after 1581 [112]. Altogether, 433 statutes were enacted during the reign, but about 930 bills failed. Some were rejected by the Lords or Commons and others vetoed by the Queen, but the chief reason for abortive measures was Elizabeth's preference for short parliamentary sessions. Bills simply ran out of time. And most of them began in the Commons: for example, all but one of the fifty-eight abortive bills in 1559 and 227 of the 271 in 1572–81. In the later parliaments of the reign (1584/85–1601), two-thirds of those originating in the Lower House failed to be enacted [34 *pp. 139–40*].

THE LORDS' ROLE

The number and proportion of bills which commenced in the Lords declined after its unfortunate Marian experience in 1553–55 (see pp. 15–16). No matter how they commenced – whether submitted by Councillors, bishops or boroughs, peers or ports, sectional or economic interests, or drawn up by a parliamentary committee – the House of origin was the major formative influence on the final product. It licked their contents into shape, revised and even re-drafted them in bill committees, engrossed them on parchment and refined their wording. It also acquired proprietary rights over them. The other chamber might reject them, but if not it passed them unaltered or it recommended changes to the House of origin [66 *p. 111–13*]. It could not effect such modifications itself unless it first consulted the other House or it replaced the original with a new bill, of which it was now the proprietor. Whilst it is clear that the Lords' initiating role diminished, Sir Christopher Hatton exaggerated when he wrote in 1586 that 'the use [custom] of the higher house is not to meddle with any bill until there be some presented from the commons' [71 *p. 373*]. In 1584 the Lords had initiated seventeen of the forty-eight Acts, whilst nine out of twenty-four commenced there in 1589. Of course, a quantitative assessment can be misleading. The passage of private estate bills (most of which commenced in the Commons), general pardons and restitutions in blood (which usually began in the Upper House) was in most cases a formality. In contrast, important public bills could be contentious and their parliamentary journey lengthy and hazardous. Whereas personal and local measures affected only a few, general bills could touch all. Even when these qualitative glosses are taken into account, however, there is no doubt that the Lords remained prominent in the legislative process. Indeed, from 1571 it underwent a revival and more official bills commenced there, due to the presence of Elizabeth's chief minister, Lord Burghley.

Furthermore, the Lords continued to be more productive because it was more efficient. It was superior in parliamentary skills, experience and organisation, and as it initiated fewer bills it could devote more time to each of them. In 1559 all but one of its bills became law, but only 30 per cent of Commons' measures; in 1563 success rates were 71 and 21 per cent respectively; in 1572–81 42 and 18 per cent; in 1593 71 and 30 per cent; and in 1597 52 and 25 per cent. It even played an important part in the enactment of local bills, which one might expect to have been brought in by knights or burgesses. In the parliaments of 1584–1601, for example, just over one-fifth of such bills began in the Lords and its success rate was superior to that of the Commons: 44 to 15 per cent [31; 116 *p. 158*]. Although the House of Lords continued to be an effective legislative chamber, in the later Elizabethan parliaments its political role was changing. Increasingly, it acted as an intermediary or broker, serving and representing the interests of both Crown and society. So the Lords joined with the Commons on such matters as the succession and Mary Stuart, but in 1593 it forced the Commons' hand by demanding a triple subsidy (see pp. 64–5).

THE PRIVY COUNCIL'S MANAGERIAL ROLE

Privy Councillors were not separate or different from other members of the two houses. It is true that they were bound to serve the Queen faithfully and diligently and that they were members of the chief organ of royal government. Nevertheless, the peers, gentlemen and lawyers who sat at the Council board also belonged to the governing class. They shared the political priorities, social interests, prejudices and fears of those with whom they worked in parliaments. Furthermore, many of the latter served the Crown in a variety of capacities. There was no obvious division of parliaments into Councillors and the rest, and even less into government and opposition, a notion quite alien to the sixteenth century. Opposition to particular royal actions and policies, or heated disagreements between the Queen and some members of both houses were certainly possible, and indeed sometimes they occurred. Then it was the Council's urgent priority to overcome opposition and eliminate discord. However, this tended to be an infrequent, emergency managerial function rather than a regular managerial preoccupation. For most of the time Elizabeth's Councillors worked to achieve three objectives: to obtain necessary taxes and laws; to join with the two houses in order to lobby her on specific issues; and to enable members of the governing class to realise at least some of their legislative expectations. In their attempts to juggle these competing priorities, Councillors had to contend with an imperious, obstinate royal mistress, her preference for short sessions, the many private bills, and parliamentary inefficiency [136].

Managerial activity focused on the Commons, not because it was more important or obstreperous than the Lords, but because its ineffectiveness (relative to the Lords) and its formidable volume of business threatened official objectives. Conciliar preparations began before parliaments met. Councillors produced initial drafts of crucial measures, including the subsidy bill (see p. 71). For some sessions there survive legislative programmes drawn up by William Cecil or devised by committees of lawyers appointed by the Council [66 *pp. 71–4*]. Those who were not peers secured their election in order to guide official business through the Commons, and the presence there of such respected and skilful Councillors as Hatton, Knollys, Mildmay, Walsingham and above all the Cecils, father and son, was crucial. Finally, care was taken to select a suitable Speaker, because he determined the order of the Commons' business. Theoretically, the Commons freely elected him, but once again theory and practice differed. In 1593, for example, Elizabeth and her Council chose Sir Edward Coke. When Parliament met three weeks later, a Councillor nominated him, the House elected him, and the Queen graciously approved. The presiding officer and the Councillors sitting around his chair always shared an intimate relationship. Although Elizabethan Speakers were not members of the Council, all but one were eminent lawyers, and three (Richard Onslow in 1566, John Popham in 1581 and Coke in 1593) served as Solicitor General. The sole exception, Sir Thomas Gargrave (1559), was a prominent royal official. The Speaker served the Council in various ways, by giving priority to official business and admonishing the House to avoid lengthy speeches and private matters. He could go further, as Christopher Yelverton did in 1597, twice calling for a vote to secure the passage of a bill for Sir Robert Cecil [12, VII *pp. 482–3*].

Between 1559 and 1566–67 William Cecil was the chief manager of conciliar activity. However, his elevation to the Lords required important changes in managerial techniques. Burghley used messages in the Queen's name and collective pressure from the Upper House to ensure that the Commons gave precedence to urgent public business [*Doc. 35*]. Naturally he looked to his fellow Councillors there, but with his departure his men-of-business also sprang into prominence. They were a motley collection of clients, careerists and devoted loyalists, but they also shared common characteristics. They were not prominent politicians of the first rank. Whilst some of them occupied municipal positions, they did not hold offices in royal government and so were 'independent' or 'private' men. Professor Collinson's concept of men-of-business extends to include secondary office-holders such as Robert Beale, Clerk to the Privy Council, and James Morrice, who was one of Burghley's subordinates in the Court of Wards [131 *pp. 191–2*]. Many of the men-of-business had connections with Burghley. Thomas Dannett (his distant relative and the Earl of Leicester's servant) and Thomas Norton (his client) assisted in the succession campaign of 1563–66/67. With Thomas Digges (a client of Burghley's ally, Lord Keeper Bacon) they bayed for the deaths of Mary Stuart and the Duke of Norfolk in 1572. Later on, Digges became noted for hurrying the Commons along and terminating prolonged debates [133 *pp. 19, 24, 31*].

The most important conciliar aides were the careerist lawyers and London's members. The former included four Commons' Speakers and Thomas Wilbraham who was prominent in 'the great cause' in 1572. For lawyers such as Robert Bell (with Bacon connections), Popham and Yelverton, the Speakership was the first upward step towards high judicial office [133 *pp. 19–20, 25, 31*]. The City's members had important business links with the Privy Council and acted as intermediaries between the two, whilst William Fleetwood, like Norton, was Burghley's client. Amongst the men-of-business, Norton had no equal. Until his death in 1584 he served the Council as an expert parliamentary draftsman, active committee man, procedural innovator and impressive debater [96 *pp. 19–34*; 97]. Both during his life and posthumously, he was known as 'Master Norton the Parliament man' [97 *pp. 1, 388, 410*]. Finally, there were the Commons' Clerks, especially Fulk Onslow who provided Burghley with reports on parliamentary proceedings.

It was no coincidence that in 1571, when Burghley took his seat in the Lords, Norton and Fleetwood became important City officials with assured seats in the Commons, Fulk Onslow was appointed Clerk, and Sir Thomas Smith, Burghley's trusted friend, was returned for Essex, whilst in 1572 Bell was chosen Speaker. The Lord Treasurer's attempt to place reliable lieutenants was typically thorough. Not that they were always reliable. They could be independent, brash, even rash. Sometimes Fleetwood's lengthy speeches and the London members' duty to advance City interests hindered rather than helped. Worse still, they could stray from customary circumspection to indiscretion and so incur royal disapproval. Norton and James Dalton spent time in the Tower for their outspoken opposition to the Queen's intended marriage to the Duke of Anjou. In 1593 Beale and Morrice were penalised for their religious zeal. Nevertheless, even if the men-of-business fell short of perfection, they served Burghley well. They promoted conciliar designs of which the Queen would not have approved; they strove to improve the Commons' efficiency; and they introduced time-saving devices. Through their efforts the House regularised joint conferences with the Lords, approved afternoon sittings for private bills, sorted measures into an order of priority, and used committees to get private business off the floor of the House [133 *pp. 15–16*]. Furthermore, specialist committees dealt with particular problems, such as timber preservation and cloth, which spawned many bills [96 *pp. 24–5*]. The men-of-business also served as Burghley's eyes and ears. Onslow (in 1572, 1581 and 1586/87), anonymous reporters and advisers (in 1572 and 1584/85), and Thomas Cromwell, Digges, William Fitzwilliam and Fleetwood (in the 1580s) kept him informed on Commons' proceedings [133 *pp. 30, 32; 26 pp. 266–7*].

Although Norton was always in the thick of things, he was not unique. However, his words must stand as the watchword of Burghley's men-of-business: '[A]ll that I have done I did by commandment of . . . the Queen's council there, and my chiefest care was in all things to be directed by the council' [97 *p. 386*]. By enlisting the help of the Queen, Lords, fellow Councillors, and men-of-business, Burghley was able to guide official business through Parliament. And, so long as he sat in the Upper House, the centre of parliamentary gravity was there. In the later years of the reign, however, the role and importance of the men-of-business may have diminished. Crucial issues had been resolved by time (in the case of the Queen's marriage) or (when Mary Stuart was executed) by success. During the long war with Spain, Parliament was called chiefly for money and there was not the same need for such activists. Dannett, Digges, Cromwell and Dalton sat in their last parliaments in 1572, 1584, 1589 and 1593 respectively. Norton died in 1584 and Fleetwood retired as London's Recorder in 1592. They had no obvious replacements. The Privy Council was served instead by ambitious career-lawyers, such as John Puckering, Thomas Egerton, Edward Coke and John Popham, who were *en route* to high judicial offices and seats as legal assistants in the House of Lords. Finally, in 1601, after Burghley's death, the centre of parliamentary gravity shifted back to the Commons, where his political heir, Sir Robert Cecil, sat and assumed responsibility for management.

PART THREE: ASSESSMENT

8 CONCLUSION

In his study of *The Evolution of Parliament*, published in 1920, A.F. Pollard identified the consolidation of the House of Commons as the most important development in the parliamentary history of the sixteenth century. It acquired a corporate consciousness, superseded the Lords, and became the focus of parliamentary activity. His pupil and successor, Sir John Neale, elaborated upon this theme, detected a growing, Commons-based opposition to royal authority and postulated the thesis that the origins of the English Civil War were to be found in the Elizabethan parliaments. Thus there was created a coherent, consistent and well-rounded picture of a rising Parliament and, within it, a politically maturing House of Commons which was becoming more disposed and able to criticise, oppose and challenge the Crown. This thesis had a seductive quality because it was consistent with events during the forty years after Elizabeth's death – or at least with the views of early Stuart historians who wrote at the same time as Pollard and Neale. In contrast, the well-established interpretation which they overthrew was certainly not in harmony with either pre- or post-Tudor developments. It can be summarised briefly. The long-term rise of Parliament was interrupted when fifteenth-century Lancastrian constitutionalism gave way to the strong 'New Monarchy' of the Yorkists and Henry VII. Sixteenth-century government was characterised by submissive parliaments and autocratic Tudor rulers. In 1603 this lengthy aberration ended and Parliament resumed its upward progress which culminated in the neutralisation of the monarchy, the political castration of the Lords, adult suffrage and the Commons' supremacy during the nineteenth and twentieth centuries.

The new interpretation fitted neatly into this scheme. Moreover, its adherents were conscious of the need to see the Tudor parliaments in the context of what came before, and especially of what happened afterwards. So Neale searched for the origins of seventeenth-century conflict, whilst Wallace Notestein, an American historian working in the same field, was one of the few (then or since) to produce a parliamentary study which did not stop or start in 1603 [73]. There are elements of truth in their thesis of a rising Parliament and they should not be dismissed lightly. The sovereignty of King-in-Parliament and the supremacy of statute were products of the sixteenth century, whilst the monopolies uproar in 1601 demonstrated how a united House of Commons could extract concessions from a Tudor monarch. Nevertheless, their political interpretation has come under serious attack from revisionist historians during the past fifteen years and it is not difficult to see why. Pollard, Neale, Notestein and others fell into the trap of trying to explain seventeenth-century upheavals, instead of studying Tudor parliaments in their own right and not as a mere prologue. They imposed upon their material a preconception, which in turn determined their treatment of parliaments in political terms. Their own historical training reinforced this approach. Pollard's apprenticeship was as a contributor to the *Dictionary of National Biography,* and thereafter his best pieces were the biographical studies of great men (see pp. 20–1). Likewise, Neale won acclaim for his life of Queen Elizabeth I and later he became editor of the Elizabethan volumes of the *History of Parliament.* This was a misnomer, because it consisted of no more than a collection of constituency surveys and biographies of knights and burgesses in the Commons. It was not an institutional study and it excluded the House of Lords. The political-cum-biographical approach to Tudor parliaments, combined with the concentration on the Commons and the concern to relate them to Stuart developments, dictated the priorities of the political school.

The whiggish interpretation of Pollard and Neale marked them off as men of their times. The Tudor revisionists are no less creatures of circumstances, responding to both particular and general contemporary influences such as G.R. Elton's institutional, archival and administrative emphases [66; 75; 76; 77], and the impact of the human sciences, which first expressed itself in Elizabethan and early Stuart county and urban studies. They have moved away from kings and queens, great politicians and high political drama, and asked new questions: how did the institution of Parliament work? what was its business? and how did it relate to the community in which its members lived? These were questions to which the political school supplied few answers. Much of Neale's supposed institutional study of the House of Commons was devoted to the politics of its elections and biographical information about its members [71]. Although Pollard published articles on the clerical organisation of Parliament [86; 87; 88], as well as *The Evolution of Parliament* [35], he was less fluent, often obscure, and at times almost incomprehensible when he turned from biography to the history of an institution.

The revisionists, with their different priorities, have supplied some of the deficiencies of the political school. They have argued persuasively that to examine the politics of an institution without an adequate knowledge of its functions, its business, and how that business was transacted, is to put the cart before the horse. In the process they have rehabilitated the House of Lords – a sensible exercise because it was, after all, co-equal with the Commons in law-making. And they have also treated Parliament as representative of the community and reflecting its concerns, rather than as some kind of autonomous creature with a political life of its own. In all of these respects the revisionists' work represents an advance on that of the political school. As yet, however, their approach has been piecemeal rather than comprehensive. They have demolished some aspects of the older interpretation and criticised others without, as yet, providing a coherent alternative, although a number of general interim assessments have appeared in print [30; 31; 33; 34; 63; 64; 67; 68; 69; 137].

Therefore, what benefits have accrued to scholars and students of History from the labours of the revisionists? First, they have substantially proved that, whilst the authority of King-in-Parliament increased in the sixteenth century, in the short term this development augmented rather than detracted from the monarch's power. Secondly, they have convincingly rejected the notion that the Commons' political muscle and Commons-centred opposition to royal government increased – and especially that *organised* opposition was a regular feature of the Elizabethan Lower House. As we have seen, they have also restored to a prominent place the House of Lords, whose institutional authority was augmented by the presence of so many patrons with kin and clients in the Lower House.

On the other hand, there is an inherent danger in the revisionist approach: that concentration on the parochial nature of much parliamentary business and the emphasis on harmony between the Crown and governing class could sweep serious political disputes behind the door or under the carpet, as if they did not exist. Friction was seldom absent, whether it was between the Crown and members of the two houses, or between competing economic, local or sectional lobbies. But this must be seen in its right perspective. Two of the functions of Elizabethan parliaments were communication between Queen and governing class and the fulfilment of parochial expectations. If these were sometimes expressed in a fractious way, that was not necessarily harmful and could be beneficial, because parliaments were also a safety-valve, a chance to let off steam. Nevertheless, genuine political conflicts should not be explained away as occasional aberrations in an otherwise harmonious relationship, without acknowledging their true significance. The Catholics in the Upper House stoutly resisted the Elizabethan Settlement in 1559; Lords and Commons worked together in 1563–66/67 in an attempt to extract a royal declaration on the succession; the Lower House protested volubly at William Strickland's sequestration in 1571; bishops, Councillors and other members of moderate reforming persuasion sought reforms in the Church in the 1560s and 1570s; Presbyterians campaigned for major ecclesiastical changes in the 1580s; the Lords confronted the Commons with a demand for increased taxation in 1593; and the Lower House was outspoken in its condemnation of harmful monopolies in 1601. The simple fact is that the Elizabethan Lords and Commons were willing and able to challenge both the Queen and each other. To this extent the political historians were right.

On the other hand, the revisionists are not seriously astray. Despite stresses and strains, parliaments were usually co-operative and optimistic occasions. Although disagreements did occur amongst competing lobbies and interests, within each House, and between the three members of the parliamentary trinity, they usually concerned specific measures (private as well as public) and particular royal policies and actions (or, in Elizabeth's case, inaction). Dean has rightly drawn attention to the Puritans as 'an extremely active and well-organised lobby' both in Parliament and outside, but he acknowledges that even their opposition occurred within an essentially stable and consensual framework [117 *pp. 140–1, 149–51*]. There was at no time a struggle for power in the state.

Parliament was an important but irregular part of Elizabethan government. Individual parliaments were no longer merely occasions. They were meetings of an institution. G.R. Elton maintained that, although it had only an intermittent existence, the Elizabethan Parliament was undeniably an institution, because it had known routines and procedures from the moment of its summons until its dissolution [65 *p. 85*]. The duties of the Clerk of the Parliaments were not confined to the 'parliament-time' and from Henry VII's reign onwards the parliamentary archive was in permanent existence. Parliament might be compared with the central courts at Westminster, which were more often in recess than in session. Furthermore, Burghley's Interregnum bill (1584), which dealt with the succession in the event of Elizabeth's death, illustrated the enormous power which Parliament could wield in troublous times. In this case it legislated for a period in which there was no King or Queen, even though no one doubted that the monarchy was an institution. The only admissible conclusion is that Elizabethan parliaments were meetings of an undoubted institution in the structure of Tudor government, but one which was not activated often and then only for short periods. However, Elton also emphasised that the importance of this institution should not be exaggerated. Politically it was 'only a secondary instrument to be used or ignored by agencies whose real power base and arena of activity lay elsewhere – at Court or in Council' [66 *pp. 377–9*]. Even private interests – local, economic and personal – did not hold it in awe and used it as just one of a number of avenues to the achievement of their objectives (see p. 75).

It was also an institution which remained, for the most part, under some degree of conciliar guidance. Nor did that diminish as the number of Councillors who sat in the Commons declined in the later Elizabethan parliaments. This decline was partly the consequence of the shrinking Council: from eighteen in 1559 to thirteen in 1601, when only five non-noble members were eligible for election. It also reflected the Councillors' preference for management of the Commons through clients and other men-of-business. In the end, the variations in managerial techniques mattered little, because the Queen usually got what she wanted. However, sometimes she got more than she bargained for. When that occurred it was rarely a Crown-Commons confrontation. Often – especially until the execution of Mary Stuart – it was a parliamentary campaign in which the Councillors played the role of puppeteers and discreetly pulled the strings in order to coerce Elizabeth into action.

As for the respective roles of the two houses, the Commons became the chief initiator of bills and progressively increased its share of business. On the other hand, the Lords should not be dismissed as insignificant and subservient. It could display an independent temper; its moderate intermediary role should not be misread as weakness; and the peers' political influence as a social élite strengthened the collective authority of the House.

Furthermore, Burghley's presence meant that official initiatives tended to derive from there between 1571 and 1597. In the last ten to fifteen years of the reign there were ominous signs of change which might have threatened parliamentary stability: a decline in political morality; the growth of corruption; the emergence of the would-be monopolistic favourite, the Earl of Essex; the installation of a monopolistic faction in power from 1601 onwards, the Cecilians; and the ongoing problem of archaic, obsolescent and irritating methods of funding government. Yet, apart from the monopolies debate (1601), these developments had no significant impact on late Elizabethan parliaments. Even the bitter power struggle at Court between Sir Robert Cecil and Essex had no obvious parliamentary repercussions. To the very end parliaments remained conclaves of the Queen and her homogeneous governing class, and they were characterised by an essential unity of mutual self-interest and devotion to the Crown. Within that framework, friction and squabbles posed no threat of political destabilisation. Queen, Council, Lords and Commons managed to work through political crises together. However, for the most part, undramatic legislative business and productivity were the characteristics and pre-eminent concerns of Elizabethan parliaments.

PART FOUR: DOCUMENTS

The following documents serve three purposes: they illustrate the main themes of the book, introduce the reader to the sources on which any study of Elizabethan parliaments must be based, and also expose the human face of the institution. The sources included here fall into four categories. The most important are the official records which any session produced: the Lords' [*Doc. 17*] and Commons' journals [*Docs 20, 22, 23, 25, 28, 29, 35*], which were the records of business of the two houses; and the *Statutes of the Realm* [*Docs 7, 8*], the nineteenth-century printed edition of the public Acts passed by the Tudor parliaments. Sir Simonds D'Ewes's published collection of journals [*Docs 2, 3, 18, 21, 24, 26*] might be placed in this category too. Although it was not an official publication, it is the only available version of the later Elizabethan Commons' journals, which are no longer extant for the sessions between 1584 and 1601. And despite his irritating abridgement of the record with references to the reading of bills of 'no great moment', without identifying them, it is an invaluable supplement to the surviving records.

Secondly, there was the paper by-product of any Parliament, especially (but not only) during the elections, when the Council, patrons, and prospective candidates were busy writing letters in their own or the public interest [*Docs 11, 13, 14, 15, 16, 31*]. Such correspondence reveals some of the political and social interests which had an impact on both parliamentary elections and sessions. So, too, do the surviving papers of participants in Elizabethan parliaments. They range from the advices penned by an experienced Parliament-man for a Councillor [*Docs 19, 29, 34*] to speeches [*Docs 4, 5, 6, 30*] and the personal diaries and journals of curious and observant members [*Docs 10, 12, 20, 22, 23, 26, 27, 28, 33*]. Finally, there were those who wrote commentaries or descriptions of the powers, procedures and business of parliaments. On the one hand, there was Sir Thomas Smith, a man of affairs, diplomat, and Elizabeth's principal Secretary [*Docs 1, 9, 32*]. In contrast, the pinnacle of John Hooker's career was civic office in Exeter [*Doc. 9*].

The abiding impression which remains from a reading of the letters, diaries and tracts left by all kinds and degrees of Elizabethans – politicians, local gentlemen, lawyers, burgesses and antiquaries – is a devotion to the monarchy *and* a reverence for parliaments. However, it is worth remembering that these were the active enthusiasts. That is why they listened, watched and wrote down what they observed, why they made transcripts of members' speeches and carefully recorded the minutiae of parliamentary procedure and ceremonial. The history of the Elizabethan parliaments suggests that, whilst most members shared their sentiments, their devotion did not necessarily extend to hard work.

DOCUMENT 1   **SIR THOMAS SMITH ON THE LEGISLATIVE FUNCTION OF PARLIAMENT**

The Parliament abrogateth olde laws, maketh new, giveth orders for things past, and for things hereafter to be followed, changeth rights and possessions of private men, legitimateth bastards, establisheth forms of religion, altereth weights and measures, giveth forms of succession to the crown, defineth of doubtful rights, whereof is no law already made, appointeth subsidies, tailles, taxes and impositions, giveth most free pardons and absolutions, restoreth in blood and name as the highest court, condemneth or absolveth them whom the Prince will put to that trial. And to be short . . . the same may be done by the Parliament of England, which representeth and hath the power of the whole realm both the head and body . . . And the consent of the Parliament is taken to be every man's consent.

De Republica Anglorum, [19], p. 49.

DOCUMENT 2   **LORD BURGHLEY ON THE PARLIAMENTARY TRINITY, 1585**

And that the Lord Treasurer [Lord Burghley] being the chiefest of the Committees of the Lords [who had just met members of the Commons in a joint conference between the two houses], showed unto the said Committees of this House, that their Lordships of the Upper House being of such quality and calling as they are known to be are one Member of the Parliament; And also that the Knights, Citizens and Burgesses of this House representing the whole Commons of this Realm, are also another Member of the same Parliament, and her Majesty the Head; And that of these three Estates doth consist the whole Body of the Parliament able to make Laws.

Sir Simonds D'Ewes, [7], p. 350.

DOCUMENT 3   **LORD KEEPER BACON ADDRESSES PARLIAMENT, 1559**

My lords and masters all, the queen's most excellent majesty, our natural and most gracious sovereign lady, having, as you know, summoned hither her high court of parliament, hath commanded me to open and declare the chief causes and considerations that moved her highness thereunto . . . Now the matters and causes whereupon you are to consult are chiefly and principally three points. Of those the first is of well making of laws, for the according and uniting of these people of the realm into an uniform order of religion, to the honour and glory of God, the establishing of the Church, and tranquillity of the realm . . . For the first, the queen's majesty having God before her eyes, and being neither unmindful of precepts and divine councils, meaneth and intendeth in this conference, first and chiefly there should be sought the advancement of God's honour and glory, . . . whereupon the policies of every good common-wealth are to be erected and knit . . . And like as the well and perfect doing of this cannot but make good success in all the rest, so the remiss and loose dealing in this, cannot but make the rest full of imperfections and doubtfulness; which must needs bring with them continual change and alteration; things much to be eschewed in all good governances, and most of all in matters of faith and religion; which of their natures be, and ought to be, most stable.

Wherefore her highness willeth and most earnestly requireth you all . . . that in this consultation, you with all humbleness, singleness and pureness of mind, confirm yourselves together, using your whole endeavour and diligence by laws and ordinances to establish that which by your learning and wisdom shall be thought most meet for the well performing of this godly purpose . . . And therewith, that you will also in this your assembly and conference clearly forebear and, as a great enemy to good council, fly from all manner of contentions, reasonings and disputations; and all sophistical, captious and frivolous arguments and quiddities, meeter for ostentation of wit than consultation of weighty matters, comelier for scholars than counsellors; more beseeming for schools than for parliament houses. Besides that commonly they be great causes of much expense of time and breed few good resolutions. And like as in council all contention should be eschewed, even so by council provision should be made that no contentions, contumelious nor opprobrious words, as heretic, schismatic, papist and such like names, being nurses of such seditious factions and sects, be used, but may be banished out of men's mouths as the causers, continuers and increasers of displeasure, hate and malice; and as utter enemies to all concord and unity, the very marks that you are now come to shoot at.

Again . . . nothing [should] be advised or done which any way in continuance of time were likely to breed or nourish any kind of idolatry or superstition; so, on the other side, heed is to be taken that, by no licentious or loose handling, any . . . contempt or irreverent behaviour towards God and godly things or any spice of irreligion might creep in . . .

Sir Simonds D'Ewes, [7], pp. 11–12.

DOCUMENT 4   **VISCOUNT MONTAGU'S SPEECH ON THE SUPREMACY BILL: SOCIAL DISORDER AND FOREIGN THREATS, 1559**

For as in the first part the supremacy is only entreated of, even so in the body of the bill all that ever was made for the defence of the faith against the malignity of wicked heresies are wholly repealed, and the confusion lately used in religion newly received and established: the mass abrogated, the sacrifice of the Church rejected, the sacraments profaned, the holy altars destroyed, temples violated, marriage of priests allowed, their children made legitimate, liberty given to them by purchase, or other means, to procure to their posterity lands and hereditaments. And thus I conceive the effect of this bill . . .

In changing of religion we condemn all other nations, of whom some be our friends and many our enemies, open and ancient, who long time have, and no doubt do expect, an opportunity to annoy us. If the pope hearing us by schism divided from the Church do proceed to the excommunication of the realm . . . how enjoyeth the king of Spain . . . ? And thereby authority given to him to possess the same that could by strong hand obtain it? This . . . may be of right feared in ourselves, being environed [surrounded] and, as it were, set about in one of two so potent enemies, who as you know would be loath to lose such opportunity . . . And add to this our own weakness and poverty at home: men's minds discontented, great sums of money due, and more of necessity demanded; and chiefly remember the evil nature of our people that always upon a little liberty are ready to rebel . . . which thing if it do happen (as too often of late it hath done), who seeth not the peril of the realm almost inevitable?

Hartley, [10], pp. 7, 10.

DOCUMENT 5   ARCHBISHOP HEATH'S SPEECH ON THE
SUPREMACY BILL: ENGLAND'S ISOLATION
AND THE RULE OF A WOMAN, 1559

Now to the first point, wherein I promised to examine this forsaking and
fleeing from the see of Rome, what matter either of weight, danger or
inconvenience doth consist therein . . . First, we must forsake and flee from
all general councils. Secondly, we must flee from all canonical and
ecclesiastical laws of the Church of Christ. Third, from the judgement of all
other Christian princes. Fourth and last, we must forsake and flee from the
unity of Christ's Church and by leaping out of Peter's ship hazard ourselves
to be overwhelmed and drowned in the waters of schism, sects and divisions
. . . [H]er highness, being a woman by birth and nature, is not qualified by
God's words to feed the flock of Christ . . . Therefore it appeareth, that like
as your honours have not His authority to give her highness this second
point of spiritual government, to feed the flock of Christ, so by [Saint]
Paul's doctrine her highness may not intermeddle herself with the same.
Therefore she cannot be supreme head of Christ's Church here in this realm
. . . [T]o preach or minister the holy sacraments a woman may not; neither
may she be supreme head of the Church of Christ.

John Strype, *Annals of the Reformation*, Oxford, vol. I, pt ii, pp. 399–407,
1824.

DOCUMENT 6   ABBOT FECKENHAM'S SPEECH: SOCIAL
DISORDER, 1559

Touching the . . . putting of difference between these religions, it is to be
considered of your honours which of them both doth breed more obedient,
humble and better subjects, first and chiefly unto our saviour and redeemer,
secondly unto our sovereign lady the queen's highness and to all other
superiors. And for some trial and probation thereof, I shall desire your
honours to consider the sudden mutation of the subjects of this realm since
the death of good Queen Mary, only caused in them by the preachers of
this new religion, when in Queen Mary's days your honours do know right
well how the people of this realm did live in an order and would not run
before laws, nor openly disobey the queen's highness' proceedings and
proclamations. There was no spoiling of churches, pulling down of altars,
and most blasphemous treading of sacraments under their feet, and hanging
up the knave of clubs in the place thereof. There was no . . . cutting of the
faces and legs of the crucifix and image of Christ. There was no open flesh
eating . . . in Lent and days prohibited . . . And now, since the coming and
reign of our most sovereign and dear lady Queen Elizabeth, by the only

preachers and scaffold players of this new religion, all things are turned upside-down . . . obedience is gone, humility and meekness clear abolished, virtuous chastity and straight living denied as though they had never been heard of in this realm . . .

John Strype, *Annals of the Reformation*, Oxford, vol. I, pt ii, p. 436, 1824.

DOCUMENT 7   HENRY VIII AND THE ROYAL
             SUPREMACY, 1534

Albeit the King's Majesty justly and rightfully is and oweth to be the supreme head of the Church of England . . . yet nevertheless for corroboration and confirmation thereof . . . Be it enacted by authority of this present Parliament that the King our sovereign lord, his heirs and successors kings of this realm, shall be taken, accepted and reputed the only supreme head in earth of the Church of England . . . and shall have and enjoy annexed and united to the imperial crown of this realm . . . full power and authority from time to time to visit, repress, redress, reform, order, correct, restrain and amend all such errors, heresies, abuses, offences, contempts and enormities . . .

26 Henry VIII, Cap. 1. From *The Statutes of the Realm*, [16], vol. III, p. 492.

DOCUMENT 8   ELIZABETH I AND THE ROYAL
             SUPREMACY, 1559

May it therefore please your Highness . . . that it may be enacted by the authority of this present Parliament . . . that your Highness, your heirs and successors, kings or queens of this realm, shall have full power and authority, by virtue of this act . . . to assign, name and authorise . . . such person or persons being natural born subjects to your Highness, your heirs or successors, as your Majesty, your heirs or successors, shall think meet, to exercise . . . all manner of . . . spiritual or ecclesiastical jurisdiction within these your realms . . . and to visit, reform, redress, order, correct and amend all such errors, heresies, schisms, abuses, offences, contempts and enormities whatsoever . . .

1 Elizabeth I, Cap. 1. From *The Statutes of the Realm*, [16], vol. IV, pp. 351, 352.

DOCUMENT 9 **(a) SIR THOMAS SMITH'S DESCRIPTION OF THE ELIZABETHAN PARLIAMENT HOUSE**

The place where the assembly is, is richly tapessed and hanged,[1] a princely and royal throne as appertaineth to a king, set in the midst of the higher place thereof. Next under the prince sitteth the chancellor, who is the voice and orator of the prince. On the one side of that house or chamber sitteth the archbishops and bishops, each in his rank, on the other side the dukes and barons.[2] In the midst thereof upon woolsacks sitteth the judges of the realm, the master of the rolls, and the secretaries of state. But these that sit on the woolsacks have no voice in the house, but only sit there to answer their knowledge in the law, when they be asked if any doubt arise among the lords. The secretaries to answer of such letters or things passed in council whereof they have the custody and knowledge: and this is called the upper house . . .

De Republica Anglorum, [19], pp. 50–1.

[1] Hung with tapestries

[2] And also the other ranks of peerage: marquesses, earls and viscounts. Transverse benches were placed across the lower end of the chamber to accommodate the overflow of barons.

(b) ANOTHER DESCRIPTION

[The lord chancellor] hath before him his two clerks sitting at a table before them, upon which they do write and lay their books. In the middle room beneath them sit the chief justices and judges of the realm, the barons of the exchequer, the king's serjeants and all such as be of the king's learned counsel, either in common laws of the realm or of ye ecclesiastical laws, and all these sit upon great woolsacks, covered with red cloth.

John Hooker, [13], fol. 20v.

DOCUMENT 10 **THE RESIDENTIAL QUALIFICATION OF MEMBERS: A DEBATE, 1571**

Mr. Warnecombe (Hereford) against the bill:
[I]t behove all those which were burgesses to see to that bill, for (quoth he) this may touch [and] overreach their whole liberties . . . but that lords' letters shall from henceforth bear all the sway; and to this effect was all that he said.

Mr. Norton (London) for the bill:

Mr. Norton first made explanation of the meaning of the bill to be (as he said) to shame the imperfection of choice, which is too often seen, by sending of unfit men, and lest haply anything might be objected to the imperfection of the parliaments, which may seem to be scant sufficient by reason of the choice made by boroughs, for the most part, of strangers, whereas by the positive law no men ought to be chosen burgesses for any boroughs but very residents and inhabitants. He said further that the choice should be of such as were able and fit for so great a place and employment, without respect of privilege of place or degree, for that by reason of his being a burgess it might not be intended or thought he was anything the wiser.

An anonymous member against the bill:

I run wholly with the pretence of the bill that boroughs decayed may be eased or relieved . . . [but] if they be decayed then it is most fit for them that of their own company there may be some who . . . can best make relation of their state and knowing their country may devise and advise of such helps as . . . may restore the old ruins.

What was done a hundred years since I may tell safely . . .: a duke of [t]his realm wrote his prayers to a city which I know, to this effect, whereby he did signify that a parliament was to be summoned in short time and that for great causes, he was to crave aid of all his friends and, reckoning them amongst the rest, he wished them of four under nominated to choose two . . . Surely law is the only fortress of the inferior sort of people and contrary to the law the greater sort will not desire or expect anything. [I]t is further said in some towns there are not men of discretion fit: they be not the wiser (said the gentleman which spake before), for that they are burgesses . . . I mean it not so strictly that those who should be chosen should of necessity be dwellers in the town, but to be either of the town or towards the town, borderers and near neighbours at the least . . .

Anonymous Remembrances, [3], fols 157v–160v.

DOCUMENT 11   A PRIVY COUNCIL LETTER CONCERNING THE ELECTION OF BURGESSES

22 August 1597

[H]er majesty, meaning to have this her intended parliament to be served with men of understanding and knowledge for the particular estate of the places whereunto they ought to be chosen . . ., hath commanded us of her privy council to admonish you to whom her majesty's writs of summons are now directed to have good regard how this her majesty's good meaning may be observed and fulfilled. And to that intent, though we doubt not much but the principal persons of that county will have good regard to make choice without partiality or affection . . . of men meet for all good respects to serve as knights for that shire, yet in the choice of burgesses for borough towns . . . we doubt (except better regard be had herein than commonly hath been) there will be many unmeet men and unacquainted with the state of the boroughs named thereto. [A]nd therefore we require you . . . to inform [boroughs] . . . of the contents of this her majesty's good meaning for the choice of persons meet for the service of the said boroughs . . . which if it shall otherwise appear to be evil supplied, we shall have occasion to enquire and find out by whose default the same hath happened.

J. R. Dasent (ed.), *Acts of the Privy Council*, vol. XXVII, p. 361, London, 1880–1907.

DOCUMENT 12   A MEMBER REBUFFED BY SIR ROBERT CECIL, 1601

If any that sit next the door be desirous to sit next the chair, to give his opinion, I will not only give him my place, but thank him to take my charge. [This was conceived to be spoken of Sir Edward Hoby, who coming to sit near the chair, and none giving him place, sat next the door.] We that sit here, take your favours out of courtesy, not out of duty.

Hayward Townshend, [20], p. 199.

DOCUMENT 13   THE PRIVY COUNCIL'S INTERVENTION AT GATTON IN 1586

After my very hearty commendations, whereas my lords of the council do understand that Mistress Copley hath the nomination of the two burgesses for the town of Gatton, being a parcel of her jointure, it is not thought convenient, for that she is known to be evil affected, that she should bear any sway in the choice of the said burgesses. Her majesty's pleasure being such, as by our letters hath been signified unto you, that a special choice should be had for this present parliament of fit persons known to be well affected in religion and towards the estate. Their lordships have thought good therefore you should recommend unto the said burghers William Waad, one of the clerks of her majesty's privy council, and Nicholas Fuller, a counsel at the law, whom if they shall not be willing to make choice of for their burgesses, at the least you must see that care be had that there may discreet persons be chosen and well affected . . .

Your loving friend
Francis Walsingham

To my very loving friends Sir William More and Sir Thomas Browne, knights, and Richard Bostock, esq.

A. J. Kempe, *The Loseley Manuscripts*, pp. 242–3, London, 1836.

DOCUMENT 14   **PATRONS AND PARLIAMENTARY BOROUGHS**

Sir Thomas Heneage, Chancellor of the Duchy of Lancaster, and the city of Salisbury, 17 January 1593

After my very hearty commendations, her majesty for some important causes concerning the state of this her realm hath summoned a parliament: wherefore in regard I am your officer[1] and would be glad to show myself helpful towards your town upon all occasions, I have thought good earnestly to pray you that the nomination of one of your burgesses maybe left unto myself, who will care for the good of that incorporation, and place such a one therein as shall be both sound in religion and otherwise so meet a man for that incorporation's good as any you can make choice of. So shall you ease the town of half your charge, and make [me] beholding unto you for this courtesy . . . Your very loving friend, Thomas Heneage.

Historical Manuscripts Commission, 55, Various Collections, IV, p. 230.

The second Earl of Bedford, lord lieutenant of Exeter, and the city of Exeter, 30 November 1562

I thought I had for my goodwill towards you somewhat better deserved than in so trifling a matter to have such a repulse. If Mr. Malet do desire and obtain the place I shall be the better willing, and so being loath to trouble you I bid you farewell.

Historical Manuscripts Commission Reports, vol. 73, p. 43, City of Exeter, 1916.

[1] Heneage was high steward of Salisbury. He failed to secure the nomination which he sought.

DOCUMENT 15   **A PRIVY COUNCIL LETTER TO LOCAL OFFICIALS, 1571**

[U]pon some deliberation had by her majesty with us . . . her majesty hath called to her remembrance (which also we think to be true) that though the greater number of knights, citizens and burgesses for the more part are duly and orderly chosen, yet in many places such consideration is not usually had . . . to choose persons able to give good information and advice for the places for which they are nominated . . . But contrariwise that many in late parliaments (as her majesty thinketh) have been named, some for private respects and favour upon their own suits, some to enjoy some immunities from arrests upon actions during the time of the parliaments, and some other to set forth private causes by sinister labour and frivolous talks and arguments, to the prolongation of time without just cause, and without regard to the public benefit and weal of the realm; and therefore her majesty, being very desirous to have redress herein, hath charged us to devise some speedy good ways for reformation hereof at this time . . .

Matthew Parker, *Correspondence* in Bruce J. and Perrowne T. T. (eds), Parker Society, pp. 379–81, Cambridge, 1853.

DOCUMENT 16   A ROYAL LICENCE OF ABSENCE,
               1 JANUARY 1559

Right trusty and well-beloved, we greet you well. Whereas we are informed that by reason of sickness, you are not able to make your repair hither to this our sessions of parliament, to be holden at Westminster, we have thought good by these our letters to dispense with you for your absence, and do license you to remain still at home for this time. So nevertheless that you send up your proxy to some such personage, as may for you and in your name give his voice, assent, or denial to such matters as shall be treated and concluded upon in our said parliament, and these our letters patents shall be your warrant in this behalf.

Sir Simonds D'Ewes, [7], p. 3.

DOCUMENT 17   THE LORDS' ADMONITION TO
               ABSENTEES, 1597

14 November
The lord treasurer (Burghley] moved the house, that such lords as were absent from the parliament and had not sent their proxies, and such others as had made their appearance in the beginning of the parliament, and have since neglected their attendance, may be admonished to reform the same.

19 November
The lord marquess [of Winchester] desires to be excused of his attendance, by reason of his sickness, certified by the lord treasurer and earl of Shrewsbury.

The bishop of Chichester desires to be excused, by reason of sickness, certified by the bishop of Norwich.

Report made by the lord keeper, that the earl of Essex received not his writ of summons until yesterday (through the negligence of the messenger unto whom the same was delivered); and now his lordship, wanting [lacking] his health to give his attendance, desireth to be excused for his absence, the earls of Worcester and Southampton testifying his sickness.

Lords' Journals, [15], vol. II, pp. 196, 198.

DOCUMENT 18   A HYPOCRITICAL LAWYER

11 February 1585

Upon a motion made by Mr. Recorder [William Fleetwood, legal counsel and magistrate of the City of London], that those of this house towards the law, being the most part of them at the bars in her majesty's courts attending their clients' causes and neglecting the service of this house, be called by the serjeant to repair unto this house presently, and to give their attendance in the service of the same, it was ordered: that the serjeant of this house do forthwith repair unto all the said courts and there give notice and charge from this house, that all those of this house that are in any the same courts . . . shall presently make their repair unto this house, and give their attendance here . . .

Upon a motion made by Sir William Herbert that Mr. Recorder of London who erst [earlier] made a motion to this house, that those of the law being members of this house and then attending at the bars in the courts in the Hall [Westminster Hall] might be sent for to give their attendance here in this house, being now since their coming in gone out of the house himself and . . . was presently pleading at the common pleas bar [the court which handled civil lawsuits between party and party], to the great abuse of this whole house, might be forthwith sent for by the serjeant to answer his said contempt.

Sir Simonds D'Ewes, [7], p. 347.

DOCUMENT 19   ADVICE TO A COUNCILLOR AND A
                THRUST AT LAWYERS, 1572

[The anonymous adviser warned against 'motions without book for matter', i.e. unprepared, spontaneous motions, because] direct opening of them maketh disputations. The best delivering the house of them is presently to require the party to confer with some other and to bring his motion in writing, and if any offer to make speech in it, then to join him for penning it with the first motioner. The more committees[1] that you make in any case the longer it will be ere the matter come in again, *specially if you will appoint lawyers in term time.*

British Library, Harleian MS 253, [1], fols 33v, 34v–35.

---

[1] Committee members

DOCUMENT 20   THE COSTS OF ABSENTEEISM

9 November 1566

It is ordered that if, after the reading of the first bill, any of the house depart before the rising of Mr. Speaker, without licence of Mr. Speaker, to pay to the poor men's box fourpence.

4 April 1571

It is agreed upon the motion of Mr. Speaker that the Litany shall be said every day in this house during this parliament . . . and also a prayer by Mr. Speaker, such as he shall think fittest for this time, to be begun every day at half hour after eight of the clock in the morning; and that each one of this house, then making default, shall forfeit for every time 4d to the poor men's box.

18 March 1581

It is ordered and resolved by this house . . . that every knight for the shire, that hath been absent this whole session of parliament, without excuse allowed by this house, shall have . . . twenty pounds for a fine set and assessed upon him to her majesty's use, for such his default; and for and upon every citizen [or] burgess . . . for the like default ten pounds. And for some mild and favourable course of dealing to be used, by way of admonition or warning . . . it is now ordered that all such . . . as have been here and attended, at any time this session of parliament, and have departed without licence of this house shall, for his and their such default, forfeit and lose the benefit of having or receiving his or their wages, due . . . for his or their attendance in that behalf.

1 December 1601

Mr. Wiseman moved the house to remember . . . that where heretofore a collection had been used for the poor; that those which went out of the town before the parliament ended would ask leave of the Speaker and pay his money.

Commons' Journals, [21], pp. 76, 82, 136; Hayward Townshend, [20], p. 269.

DOCUMENT 21   ANTHONY COPE'S BILL AND BOOK, 1586–87

Mr. Cope, first using some speeches touching the necessity of a learned ministry . . . offered to the house a bill and a book written, the bill containing a petition that it might be enacted that all laws now in force touching ecclesiastical government should be void. And that it might be enacted that that book of common prayer now offered and none other might be received into the Church to be used. The book contained the form of prayer and administration of sacraments with divers rites and ceremonies to be used in the Church and desired that the book might be read. Whereupon Mr. Speaker in effect used this speech: for that her majesty before this time had commanded the house not to meddle with this matter, and that her majesty had promised to take order in those causes, he doubted not but to the good satisfaction of all her people, he desired that it would please them to spare the reading of it. Notwithstanding the house desired the reading of it. Whereupon Mr. Speaker willed the clerk to read it . . . Mr. Dalton made a motion against the reading of it, saying that it was not meet to be read . . . and thought that this dealing would bring her majesty's indignation against the house thus to enterprise the dealing with those things which her majesty especially had taken into her own charge and discretion. Whereupon Mr. Lewknor spake, showing the necessity of preaching and of a learned ministry, and thought it very fit that the petition and book should be read.

To this purpose spake Mr. Hurleston and Mr. Bainbridge, and so the time being passed the house broke up and the petition nor book read. This done her majesty sent to Mr. Speaker as well for this petition and book, as for that other petition and book . . . that was delivered the last session of parliament.

On Wednesday . . . Mr. Wentworth delivered unto Mr. Speaker certain articles which contained questions touching the liberties of the house . . . These questions Mr. Puckering pocketed up and showed Sir Thomas Heneage, who so handled the matter that Mr. Wentworth went to the Tower, and the questions not at all moved.

On Thursday . . . Mr. Cope, Mr. Lewknor, Mr. Hurleston and Mr. Bainbridge were sent for to my lord chancellor and by divers of the privy council, and from thence were sent to the Tower.

Sir Simonds D'Ewes, [7], pp. 410–11.

DOCUMENT 22   THE PUNISHMENT OF 'STRANGERS' BY
                THE COMMONS

(a)
23 January 1581: an interloper taken
The serjeant of this house apprehended one William Hannye, servant to Anthony Kyrle of the middle temple, gent., sitting in this house; who being none of this house and further examined, confessed upon his knees that he had sitten there that present day, by the space of half an hour at the least; craving pardon and alleging that he knew not the orders of the house; and

was thereupon committed to the serjeant's custody, till further order should be taken with him by this house.

25 January 1581: a penitent interloper

William Hannye, being brought to the bar by the serjeant, humbly, upon his knees, submitteth himself to the grace and favour of this house, acknowledging his fault to proceed only of simplicity and ignorance. Whereupon, after some examinations, when he had willingly taken the oath against the pope's supremacy, he was remitted by the house, paying his fees.[1]

Commons' Journals, [21], pp. 118, 120.

(b)

29 February 1576: a member assaulted

[Robert Bainbridge] sheweth that one Williams, having had divers unseemly speeches concerning the state, being rebuked by him, had stricken him and drawn his dagger upon him. Upon which it was agreed that he should be sent for by the mace,[2] which was performed accordingly and he committed to the custody of the serjeant.

[1] A delinquent had to pay the serjeant twenty shillings for arresting him and thereafter ten shillings a day whilst in his custody!

[2] Since Ferrers' case (1543) offenders could be arrested by authority of the house, using the serjeant's mace as its warrant (see pp. 13, 44).

Cromwell's Journal, [6], fol. 124.

(c)

1 February 1581: disorderly servants

It is ordered that Mr. Speaker, in the name of this house, do require the warden of the Fleet [Prison], being a member of this house, that he do cause from henceforth two of his servants to attend at the stairhead, near unto the outer door of this house. And to lay hands upon two or three of such disordered serving-men or pages as shall happen to use such lewd disorder and outrage, as hath been accustomed to be exercised there this parliament time; to the end they may thereupon be brought into this house, and receive such punishment as to this house shall seem meet.

Commons' Journals, [21], p. 121.

(d)

7 November 1601: a disorderly servant with long hair

There was this day a page brought to the bar, for that yesterday Sir Francis Hastings had caused him to be committed: For that as he went down the stairs, the page offered to throng [jostle] him. Whereupon he held him till the speaker came out of the house, who did commit him to the serjeant's custody ... But this day, upon Sir Francis Hastings' entreaty, speaking very earnestly for him, and of his innocency ... as also upon the page's submission upon his knees at the bar, he was discharged. It was moved that, because his hair was very long, he might be carried to a barber and close cut before his discharge. But that was thought very unfit, for the gravity of the house, to take notice of so light a fault. So, after a sharp and threatening admonition given him by the speaker, he was discharged.

Hayward Townshend, [20], pp. 195–6.

DOCUMENT 23   (a) THE INJUSTICE OF PRIVILEGE, 1559

John Smith, returned burgess for Camelford in Cornwall, upon a declaration by Mr. Marshe that he had come to this house being outlawed, and also had deceived divers merchants in London, taking wares of them to the sum of three hundred pounds, minding to defraud them of the same under the colour of privilege of this house, the examination whereof, committed to Sir John Mason and other of this house, was found and reported to be true ... Upon which matters consultation was had in the house, the question was asked by Mr. Speaker if he should have privilege of this house or not ... And upon the division of the house, the number that would have him not to have privilege was 107 persons; and the number that would he should be privileged was 112 persons; and therefore ordered that he shall still continue a member of this house.

Commons' Journals, [21], p. 55.

(b) THE PROTECTION OF PRIVILEGE, 1572

Note that during this adjournment [12–24 June] the privilege of the house was enjoyed. If any member of the parliament be arrested either in coming to the parliament or in returning from it, though the parliament be ended, he may have a special writ out of the clerk of the crown's office for his discharge.

Anonymous Journal, [2], fol. 62v.

(c) A TAILOR-MADE CASE OF PRIVILEGE, 1601

Sir Edward Hoby moved the house, that forasmuch as the ancient custom of the parliament had been that not only themselves but their servants should be free from all arrests, yet notwithstanding a servant of Mr. William Cook, a member of this house, was arrested by one Baker, a serjeant, at the suit of another, upon a bond in which indeed he is but surety . . . Upon which motion . . . it was generally agreed that the serjeant of this house should be presently sent with his mace for the said prisoner and his keeper . . . so, after the serjeant had been away about an hour and an half, he brought the prisoner and his keeper to the bar . . . And the keeper was commanded to deliver his prisoner to the serjeant, which he did . . . And the house commanded the keeper to take no fees and so the prisoner was quite discharged. But Sir Robert Wroth moved to know whether Mr. Cook would affirm that man to be his servant, who stood up and said, *He was one of his most necessary servants, for, in truth* (quoth he) *he is my tailor.*

Hayward Townshend, [20], p. 196.

DOCUMENT 24   A CASE OF PRIVILEGE DENIED, 1584

Roger Vanconge, a Dutchman and merchant stranger, being this day brought by the serjeant to the bar for arresting of John Werrall, servant unto Thomas Poole esquire, a member of this house, for debt . . .; and the said John Werrall being also brought to this house, it was after several examinations had by this house . . . resolved, after the doubtfulness of the greater number of voices upon the question, by the division of the house, that the said John Werrall should not have privilege of this house, but should . . . be remanded to the said prison . . . for that it did manifestly appear unto this house . . . that fraudulently . . . he procured himself to be received into the service of the said Mr. Poole this parliament time to escape from arrests, to the delaying and defeating of his creditors; upon which dividing of the house there were with the Yea . . . eighty-five voices and with the No but sixty-nine.

Sir Simonds D'Ewes, [7], p. 373.

DOCUMENT 25   ARTHUR HALL, 1581

4 February

Upon a motion made unto this house by Mr. Norton, in which he declared that some person of late had caused a book to be set forth in print, not only greatly reproachful against some particular good members of this house of great credit, but also very much slanderous and derogatory to the general authority, power, and state of this house, and prejudicial to the validity of the proceedings of the same, in making and establishing of laws; charging this house with drunkenness, as accompanied in their counsels with

Bacchus; and them also with choler ... [H]e conjectured the same to be done and procured by Mr. Arthur Hall, one of this house, and so prayed that thereupon the said Mr. Hall might be called by this house to answer ... And then immediately Mr. Secretary Wilson thereupon did signify unto this house that the said Mr. Hall had, upon his examination therein before the lords of the council heretofore, confessed in the hearing of the said Mr. Secretary that he did cause the said book to be printed indeed. Upon relation whereof, and after some speech also then uttered unto this house by Mr. Chancellor of the Exchequer [Sir Walter Mildmay] of the dangerous and lewd contents of the said book, the serjeant was forthwith, by order of this house, sent to apprehend the said Arthur Hall.

14 February
Mr. Vicechamberlain [Sir Christopher Hatton] for himself and the residue of the committees appointed to examine Mr. Hall ... declared that they had charged the said Mr. Hall with contempt against this house the last session ... and charged him further with divers articles of great importance, selected by the said committees out of the said book: as, first, with publishing the conferences of this house abroad in print and that, in a libel ... and containing matter of infamy of sundry good particular members of the house, and of the whole state of the house in general, and also of the power and authority of this house ... And was further charged that he had injuriously impeached the memory of the late speaker, deceased ... and that, in defacing the credit of the body and members of this house, he practised to deface the authority of the laws and proceedings in the parliament, and so to impair the ancient orders touching the government of the realm and rights of the house and the form of making laws, whereby the subjects of the realm are governed ... Unto all which things, as the said Mr. Hall could make no reasonable answer or denial, so the said Mr. Vicechamberlain, very excellently setting forth the natures and qualities of the said offences in their several degrees, moveth in the end that Mr. Hall, being then without at the door, might be called in to answer unto those points ... And that done [he] was sequestered.

Commons' Journals, [21], pp. 122, 125.

DOCUMENT 26   (a) **PAUL WENTWORTH AND THE LIBERTIES OF THE COMMONS, 1566**

Paul Wentworth, a burgess of the house, by way of motion, desired to know whether the queen's command and inhibition, that they should no longer dispute of the matter of succession (sent yesterday to the house) were not against the liberties and privileges of the said house? And thereupon arose divers arguments, which continued from nine of the clock in the morning till two of the clock in the afternoon . . . And, as it should seem, no certain resolution of the house given therein.

On Tuesday the 12th day of November, Mr. Speaker . . . began to show that he had received a special command from her highness to this house, notwithstanding her first commandment that there should not be further talk of that matter in the house . . . and if any person thought himself not satisfied, but had further reasons, let him come before the privy council and there show them.

Sir Simonds D'Ewes, [7], p. 128.

(b) PETER WENTWORTH ON THE LIBERTIES OF THE COMMONS, 1571

Mr. Wentworth very orderly in many words remembered the speech of Sir Humphrey Gilbert, delivered some days before. He proved his speech (without naming him) to be an injury to the house. He noted his disposition to flatter or fawn on the prince, comparing him to the chameleon, who can change himself into all colours saving white; even so, said he, this reporter can change himself to all fashions but honesty. He showed further the great wrong done to one of the house by a misreport made to the queen . . . He showed his speech to tend to no other end than to inculcate fear into those which should be free. He requested care for the credit of the house and for the maintenance of free speech (the only means of orderly proceedings) and to preserve the liberty of the house to reprove liars, inveighing greatly out of the scriptures and otherwise against liars.

Anonymous Remembrances, [3], fol. 167v.

(c) PETER WENTWORTH'S OFFENSIVE SPEECH, 1576

First, all matters that concern God's honour through free speech shall be propagated here and set forward and all things that do hinder it removed, repulsed and taken away. Next, there is nothing commodious, profitable, or any way beneficial for the prince or State, but faithful and loving subjects will offer it in this place . . .

Amongst other, Mr. Speaker, two things do great hurt in this place, of the which I do mean to speak: the one is a rumour which runneth about the house and this it is, 'Take heed what you do, the queen's majesty liketh not such a matter. Whosoever preferreth it, she will be offended with him'. Or the contrary, 'Her majesty liketh of such a matter. Whosoever speaketh against it, she will be much offended with him'.

The other: sometimes a message is brought into the house, either of commanding or inhibiting, very injurious to the freedom of speech and consultation. I would to God, Mr. Speaker, that these two were buried in hell, I mean rumours and messages, for wicked undoubtedly they are. The reason is, the devil was the first author of them, from whom proceedeth nothing but wickedness ...

Upon this speech the house, out of a reverent regard of her majesty's honour, stopped his further proceeding before he had fully finished his speech. Mr. Wentworth being sequestered the house ... it was agreed and ordered by the house upon the question (after sundry motions and disputations had therein) that he should be presently committed to the serjeant's ward as prisoner, and so remaining should be examined upon his said speech for the extenuating of his fault therein.

This day Mr. Treasurer [Sir Francis Knollys] in the name of all the committees yesterday appointed for the examination of Peter Wentworth ... touching the violent and wicked words yesterday pronounced by him in this house touching the queen's majesty, made a collection of the same words, which words so collected the said Peter Wentworth did acknowledge and confess.

It was ordered upon the question that the said Peter Wentworth should be committed close prisoner to the Tower for his said offence.

(d) PETER WENTWORTH'S QUESTIONS TO THE COMMONS, 1586–87

Whether this council be not a place for any member of the same here assembled, freely and without controlment of any person or danger of laws, by bill or speech to utter any of the griefs of this commonwealth whatsoever touching the service of God, the safety of the prince and this noble realm.

Whether that great honour may be done unto God, and benefit and service unto the prince and State without free speech in this council, which may be done with it.

Sir Simonds D'Ewes, [7], pp. 237, 241, 244, 411.

DOCUMENT 27   **MONOPOLIES, 1601**

20 November
Mr. Lawrence Hyde said, 'To end this controversy because the time is very short, I would move the house to have a very short bill read, entitled "an act of explanation of the common law in certain cases of letters patents" '. And all the house cried, 'I, I, I' [Aye, Aye, Aye].

Doctor Bennet [burgess for York] said, 'He that will go about to debate her majesty's prerogative royal must walk warily. In respect of a grievance out of that City for which I serve, I think myself bound to speak that now ... I mean a monopoly of salt ... Fire and water are not more necessary. But for other monopolies of cards (at which word Sir Walter Raleigh blushed), dice, starch &c. they are (because monopolies) I must confess very hateful, though not so hurtful'.

Mr. Martin [burgess for Barnstaple in Devon] said: 'I speak for a town that grieves and pines and for a country that groaneth under the burthen of monstrous and unconscionable substitutes to the monopolitans of starch, tin, fish, cloth, oil, vinegar, salt and I know not what: nay, what not? The principal commodities both of my town and country are ingrossed into the hands of these bloodsuckers of the commonwealth'.

Sir Robert Wroth said: 'I would but note Mr. Solicitor, that you were charged to take care in Hilary term last. Why not before? There was time enough ever since the last parliament. I speak it and I speak it boldly. These patentees are worse than ever they were . . . There have been divers patents granted since the last parliament; these are now in being, viz. the patents for currants, iron, powder, cards, horns, ox shin-bones . . . ashes, bottles, glasses, bags, . . . aniseed, vinegar, sea-coals, steel, aqua-vitae, brushes, pots, salt, saltpetre, lead, oil, . . . and divers others'.

Upon reading of the patents aforesaid, Mr. Hakewill of Lincoln's Inn stood up and asked this, 'Is not bread there?' 'Bread?' quoth another. 'This voice seems strange', quoth a third. 'No', quoth Mr. Hakewill, 'but if order be not taken for these, bread will be there before the next parliament'.

25 November
Mr. Speaker, after a silence (and everyone marvelling why the speaker stood up) spake to this effect: 'It pleased her majesty to command me to attend upon her yesterday . . . from whom I am to deliver unto you all her majesty's most gracious message . . . She said, that partly by intimation of her council and partly by divers petitions that have been delivered unto her, both going to chapel and also walking abroad, she understood that divers patents that she had granted were grievous unto her subjects . . . But, she said, she never assented to grant anything that was evil in itself. And if in the abuse of her grant there be anything that is evil . . . she herself would take present order for reformation thereof.'

After a little pause and silence, the council talking one with another, Mr. Secretary Cecil stood up and said . . . 'There are no patents now of force which shall not presently be revoked. For what patent soever is granted there shall be left, to the overthrow of that patent, a liberty agreeable to the law . . . I take it there is no patent whereof the execution thereof hath been injurious; would that had never been granted. I hope there shall never be more.' (All the house said, 'Amen').

Hayward Townshend, [20], pp. 230, 232, 234, 238–9, 248–9.

DOCUMENT 28   MARY STUART AND THE DUKE OF
                NORFOLK, 1572

A joint committee of the two houses devised two bills against Mary. The first and severer bill attainted her of treason and deprived her of any claim to the English crown, whereas the second simply removed her from the succession, with attainder as the penalty 'if she did proceed to any attempt hereafter'.

23 May

Mr. Comptroller [Sir James Croft], in the name of all the committees in the great Cause, declareth from her majesty, her very good and thankful acceptation of the great care of this house for her majesty's safety; and that, moved partly in conscience and partly in honour, minding to defer not to reject the determination of this house to proceed in the choice of a bill against the Scottish queen, in the highest degree of treason, both in life and title, liketh better with all convenient speed to proceed in a second bill, to the other part of the said former choice.

Commons' Journals, [21], p. 97.

Mr. Comptroller. Sheweth that he is sorry it was his chance to be the bringer of so uncomfortable a message. He would be glad if he could take away the cause of despair. He wisheth the order purposed might be proceeded in to gather the reasons of our refusal into writing. The same he hopeth will move her majesty.

Mr. Treasurer [Sir Francis Knollys]. Sithence he perceiveth all our purposes remain firm and no alteration; and sithence the queen's disposition hath been declared and not liked to be followed, it should be vain now to use any longer speeches and so to let[1] other things in proceeding. The order therefore of proceeding in this cause only to be considered. It resteth therefore to be considered whether the house think best of themselves to make petition by the mouth of their speaker to her majesty, or to move the lords to join with us in our motions as well touching the queen of Scots as the duke. He liketh best to move the lords to join with us: the request shall be more effectual.

Cromwell's Journal, [6], fols 40v–41.

24 May

After this it seemed good that a further conference should be had with the lords about this matter, which being had, it was by them agreed that every man should set down in writing such reasons as he thought were best able to move the queen herein, and that first the bishops should set down reasons moving the conscience, and next reasons for policy, in which should be answered tacitly such objections as the queen were able to make for the not proceeding in the first bill. The civilians[2] drew reasons *pro et contra*. It was agreed that the most principal reasons should be chosen and they alone set down in the writing which should be presented to the queen's majesty. It was thought better that these reasons should be thus delivered by writing rather than uttered by the mouth of any one person. For though the one way move more for the time, yet it is gone straight, and the reasons soon forgotten. Whereas the other way they are read with pausing and are considered upon, and so the better imprinted in the mind, and thereby so much the more do move.

Anonymous Journal, [2], fols 59v–60.

[1] Hinder or obstruct.

[2] Men trained in the civil law, which was practised in the Church courts, as distinct from the common law, which operated in the King's courts.

Mr. Wentworth. It remaineth yet to be considered for our petition to the queen for execution of the duke. It was determined the petition should be made by Mr. Speaker. He to think of the matter between this and Wednesday, and every man that list in the mean season to bring such allegations as they think necessary to the speaker, the same to be considered upon Wednesday and then to determine further of our proceeding.

Cromwell's *Journal*, [6], fol. 44.

31 May
Peter Wentworth moved the house to go on for motion to the queen for the execution of the duke. Snagge to the same effect. Norton to the like effect. He brought forth a paper in writing wherein he had written certain reasons which should be delivered to the speaker to be considered of, and collect the best for his purpose. Ireland to have the queen moved for the speedy execution during the session. Digges that such causes as are put in writing might be committed to certain to be allowed or disallowed of.

Onslow's *Journal*, [17], fol. 3.

25 June
Mr. Norton. The matter hath been considered by the bishops according to the word of God, by the civilians and by the judges of the common law, and all have agreed that it is just and lawful. God forbid we should prefer the vain name of honour before the safety of the queen's majesty. The example of David cannot serve. He did repent, and yet David was punished and chose himself to be rather punished than his people. The law shall protect her as long as she is obedient to law. But her title being taken away,

if she claim the crown she comes either as an enemy or a conqueror, and then by law may be killed ... He requireth that our speaker in his oration may declare to the queen's majesty that this bill is no perfect safety for the queen's majesty, but that it will be necessary for her majesty to proceed further to execution, or otherwise that both she and we shall continue in peril.

Cromwell's Journal, [6], fol. 65–65v.

DOCUMENT 29 JOINT CONFERENCES: THEIR ADVANTAGES AND DANGERS

2 May 1571. A House of Commons' resolution
[I]t is agreed that the committees for the bill against the untrue demeanours of tellers, receivers, treasurers and collectors and for the bill against bulls procured from the see of Rome, and such-like bills as hereafter shall come from their lordships, needful to be considered of, added unto, or altered, shall make request unto the lords for conference and privity in that behalf to be had and made with them as they, in the said former bill, have used and done towards this house.

Commons' Journals, [21], p. 87.

1572. Advice from an anonymous member to a Privy Councillor
I must confess that ... there is no one thing that hath so shaken the true liberty of the house as often conferences, sometimes by withdrawing the attendance of the best members among us, sometimes by terrifying of men's opinions. I mean not that the lords do terrify men, but men of the common house, coming up among them at conferences, espy their inclinations and knowing that in the common house nothing is secret, they gather other advisements [opinions], but howsoever it be, overmany conferences work many courses to prolong the session.

British Library, Harleian MS 253, [1], fol. 35v.

7 February 1581. Thomas Norton's motion
Upon a motion made by Mr. Norton, it is ordered that such persons as shall be appointed by this house, at any time, to have conference with the lords, shall and may use any reasons or persuasions they shall think good in their discretions, so as it tend to the maintenance of anything done or passed this house, before such conference had, and not otherwise; but that any such person shall not, in any wise, yield or assent [at] any such conference, to any new thing there propounded, until this house be first made privy thereof, and give such order.

Commons' Journals, [21], p. 123.

DOCUMENT 30   REQUESTS FOR SUPPLY

Lord Keeper Bacon's address to Parliament, 1563
The Queen's Majesty at her coming to the Crown [found] this her realm in a ragged and torn state . . . her frontier towns not sufficiently fortified, the revenue of the Crown greatly spoiled, the treasure of the realm not only wasted but the realm also greatly indebted; the land of Ireland much out of order; the store of all kind of munition for the realm's defence marvellously consumed; the navy and sea matters nothing in the state they now be . . . Whereupon indeed her Highness entered into the reforming and supplying of most of all those great lacks, and for the well-doing of them hath not forborne to take any care or pains, neither hath she sticked for the compassing of this both to spend her own treasure, to sell her own lands, to prove her own credit at home and abroad to the uttermost and all this for our sureties and quietness.

Sir Simonds D'Ewes, [7], pp. 192–5.

Speech of Sir Ralph Sadler, Privy Councillor, in the Commons, 1566
Surely in my poor opinion there was never greater cause why we should grant a subsidy: the necessity of the time did never more require it. For we see that the whole world, our neighbours round about us of long time have been and yet be in arms, in hostility and great garboil.[1] Only we rest here in peace and quietness, thanks be to God therefore and the good government of the Queen's Majesty. Marry it is a point of wisdom in the time of peace to provide for the war . . . [W]e hear daily of secret conspiracies and great confederacies between the Pope, the French King and other princes of the popish confederacy against all princes [who are] protestants and professors of the gospel, of the which the Queen's Majesty is the chief patroness . . . [T]herefore her Majesty never had greater cause, never more need to arm herself, to make herself strong and to furnish her coffers with treasure, whereby she may be the more able to defend her realm and subjects and to encounter and meet with the malice of her enemies.

Hartley, [10], pp. 141–4.

Sir Walter Mildmay justifies a request for a subsidy, 1576
And unless it might seem strange to some that her Majesty should want this, some considering that not long sithence aid was granted by the realm.[2] To that I answer that, albeit her Majesty is not to yield an account how she spendeth her treasure, yet for your satisfactions I will let you understand such things as are very true . . .
    First, how favourable the taxations of subsidies be through the whole realm cannot be unknown to any, whereby far less cometh to her Majesty's coffers than by the law is granted, a matter now drawn to be so usual as it is hard to be reformed. Next the clearing of all debts that run upon interest

to the insupportable charge of the realm. Thirdly, the charge in suppressing the rebellion in the North. Fourthly, the . . . honourable repayment of the last loans . . . Fifthly, the journey to Edinburgh Castle for the quieting of that country and this. And lastly, the great and continual charges in Ireland by the evil disposition of the people there. All which could not have been performed by the last Aid, except it had pleased her Majesty to spare out of her own revenues great sums of money for the supplying of that which lacked.

Sir Simonds D'Ewes, [7], pp. 244–7.

[1] Tumult or confusion.
[2] In 1571.

DOCUMENT 31 **PARLIAMENTARY TACTICS**

Geoffrey Tothill to John Hooker, chamberlain of Exeter, 31 January 1563
After my hearty commendation I have sent you herewith enclosed the copies of two bills exhibited unto the parliament house for the city, wherein I pray to God send us good success as I hope. The one, for the uniting of churches, is first in the lords house and the other for orphans in the lower house. Trusting by that time we have thoroughly considered that bill for orphans and ready to be sent off to the lords, the lords' bill will be ready to come down. I suppose the bills be indifferently handled. If we should have put both in at one place then, peradventure, the house would not be best contented with two bills for our private city. Other things in ye articles shall be remembered, as for [ap]prentices there is a bill in the parliament house for servants, which is committed to the master of the rolls and others. I hope if the bill pass to get a proviso for all cities in England to take [ap]prentices and Exeter not named. There . . . should have been this afternoon, if my leisure had served, a bill drawn for the Londoners. It shall be in the name of all the cities in the west parts and elsewhere and is not privately for us. [He desires that £10 may be] delivered to my brother Walter to be sent me, as I have retained divers in these causes and must give money about the same.

Historical Manuscripts Commission Reports, vol. 1. pp. 51–2, City of Exeter, 1916.

DOCUMENT 32   SIR THOMAS SMITH ON THE PROCEEDINGS OF THE COMMONS

In the disputing [of bills] is a marvellous good order used in the lower house. He that standeth up bareheaded is understanded that he will speak to the bill. If more stand up, who that first is judged to arise is first heard, though the one do praise the law the other dissuade it, yet there is no altercation. For every man speaketh as to the speaker, not as one to another, for that is against the order of the house.

No reviling or nipping words must be used. For then all the house will cry, 'It is against the order . . .' So that in such a multitude and in such diversity of minds and opinions, there is the greatest modesty and temperance of speech that can be used.

De Republica Anglorum, [19], pp. 54–5.

DOCUMENT 33   THOMAS NORTON AGAINST THE IRON INTEREST, 1572

Mr. Norton. The bill toucheth us all as well as the City of London, which provideth not only for itself but for the queen also and for all them which travel to the same, being no small number. It is reason all private devices give place to general commodities. The raising of the price thereof will make all other things rise for company. It hath been said it is no help for preservation of timber, but experience shall show that if coppice[1] wood be consumed the timber trees must needs be cut down for provision of fuel for the City. If it touch but one, he not to be preferred before the whole City, and now best time to provide remedy. If we tarry till 12 mills be made, there will be more criers out and harder passage. But it is no new thing that new inconveniences should have new remedies.

Sir Henry Sidney. Other occasions of the dearth of wood, besides iron mills. Iron worthy to be much made of, as we stand with other nations.

Cromwell's *Journal*, [6], fol. 33.

[1] Small trees or brushwood, grown for periodic cutting as fuel.

DOCUMENT 34   PRIVATE BILLS: THE PROBLEM AND THE ANSWER, 1572

If her majesty's meaning be to have the session short, then is it good to abridge the things that lengthen the session which, amongst others, are these.

1. The number of private bills of singular persons.
2. The bills of occupation, mysteries [guilds] and companies and specially the bills of London . . .

1. For the first matter I think good that a choice be made of bills, wherein this I note, that it is not good . . . that anything for choice or admitting or rejecting of bills to be delivered by the speaker or any councillor or other, as by her majesty's commandment. For so would by and by be raised by some humorous [difficult] body some question of the liberties of the house and of restraining their free consultation, perhaps offensive to her majesty and assuredly with long speeches to the troublesome prolonging of the session. [The writer recommended instead a tactful royal message that, in view of the members' great expenses and the approaching plague season] she will not detain them long, but the session shall be short.

This being done I wish a motion to be made presently that sithence her majesty hath so graciously made us partakers of her pleasure for shortness of the session, it shall be good for us to take our benefit of this warning for well spending and sparing our time. And therefore to pray that there may be committees of the house to consider of bills offered, to prefer the forwarding of the most necessary before the other, but in no wise to make mention of rejecting of any (although indeed it amounteth to a rejecting of those that be of small importance) for private bills ever be eagerly followed and make factions . . .

2. [T]his is the way then when any bill of London is exhibited before the open reading thereof, the knights and citizens for London be called and asked whether the matters be meet to be furthered; and also whether the same matter may not be sufficiently amended by common council or otherwise among themselves without troubling of the parliament. And if it may, then to commend it to the lord mayor and aldermen to be considered at London, and so to rid the house thereof. So shall you . . . do the City a marvellous benefit, that their matters come not too much in question, and that the reforming of their own causes be reserved to themselves.

British Library, Harleian MS 253, [1], fols 33–34v. The authorship is uncertain. A later hand on the document ascribes it to Francis Tate, a lawyer, but he did not enter parliament until 1601, and in any case he was only twelve years old in 1572. Whoever the author was, he was clearly an experienced 'Parliament man', possibly Thomas Norton. See also *Doc. 29*.

DOCUMENT 35   OFFICIAL PRESSURE ON THE COMMONS TO MAKE HASTE, 1571

In response to the Lords' request for a joint conference the Commons sent up all the Privy Councillors of the house together with sixteen other members.

21 April

[A]nd thereupon brought report to this house from the lords that, as the season of the year waxed very hot and dangerous for sickness, so they desired that this house would spend the time in proceeding with necessary bills for the commonwealth and lay aside all private bills in the meantime.

Which report was made by Mr. Treasurer and a note by him brought from the lords of such bills as they thought meetest to be treated of was read by the clerk; viz.

The bill for treasons.

For coming to the church and receiving the communion.

Against untrue demeanours of tellers, receivers and collectors.

Against such as be fled beyond seas without licence.

Against fraudulent gifts and conveyances of lands and goods.

For preservation of woods.

For respite of homage.

For corrupt returns by sheriffs.

For the subsidy.

For suits by promoters.

24 April

It is ordered by the house that a note be made against tomorrow of the titles of all the bills offered into this house and then to be read; to the end the house may make their choice with which of them they will first proceed.

26 April

The note of the titles of the bills being read, it is ordered that [15 members, including Burghley's allies, Sir Walter Mildmay and Sir Thomas Smith, and Dalton, Fleetwood, Norton and Yelverton, all clients of Councillors] shall be committees for appointing such bills for the commonweal as shall be first proceeded in and preferred before the residue, but not to reject any.

Commons' Journals, [21], pp. 85–6.

Elizabethan Parliaments

Parliament	Dates of sessions		Date of dissolution
1559		23 January–8 May 1559	8 May 1559
1563–67	(1)	11 January–10 April 1563	
	(2)	30 September 1566–	
		2 January 1567	2 January 1567
1571		2 April–29 May 1571	29 May 1571
1572–81	(1)	8 May–30 June 1572	
	(2)	8 February–15 March 1576	
	(3)	16 January–18 March 1581	19 April 1583
1584–85		23 November 1584–	
		29 March 1585	14 September 1586
1586–87		29 October 1586–23 March 1587	23 March 1587
1589		4 February–29 March 1589	29 March 1589
1593		19 February–10 April 1593	10 April 1593
1597–98		24 October 1597–	
		9 February 1598	9 February 1598
1601		27 October–19 December 1601	19 December 1601

BIBLIOGRAPHY

DOCUMENTS AND CONTEMPORARY ACCOUNTS

1. Anonymous advices to a Privy Councillor, 1572, British Library, Harleian MS, 253, fols 32–6.
2. Anonymous Journal, 8 May–25 June 1572, Bodleian Library, Tanner MS, 393, fols 45–64.
3. Anonymous 'Remembrances of the parliament', 1571, British Library, Cotton MS, Titus F.i, fols 129–71.
4. Coke, Sir Edward. *The Fourth Part of the Institutes of the Laws of England*, London, 1644.
5. Corporation of London. Repertories of the Court of Aldermen.
6. Cromwell, Thomas. *Journal of the Parliamentary Sessions of 1572–84*, Trinity College, Dublin MS, 1045, fols 1–135v.
7. D'Ewes, Sir Simonds. *The Journals of all the Parliaments during the Reign of Queen Elizabeth, both of the House of Lords and House of Commons*, London, 1682.
8. Elton, G.R. *The Tudor Constitution*, 2nd edn, Cambridge University Press, 1982.
9. Fleetwood, William. *Parliamentary diary of 1584*, British Library, Lansdowne MS, 41, fol. 45.
10. Hartley, T.E. (ed.), *Proceedings in the Parliaments of Elizabeth I*, Leicester University Press, 1981.
11. *Historical Manuscripts Commission Reports*, Duke of Rutland MS, Vols 1–4, London, 1885–1905.
12. *Historical Manuscripts Commission Reports*, Marquess of Salisbury (Hatfield) MS, Vols 1–14, London, 1883–1923.
13. Hooker, John (alias Vowell). *The Order and Usage of Parliament*, British Library, Harleian MS, 1178, no. 16, fols. 19–27.
14. Hughes, P.L. and Larkin, J.F. (eds), *Tudor Royal Proclamations*, 3 vols, New Haven and London, 1964–9.
15. *Journals of the House of Lords*, vols I, II, London, 1846.
16. Luders, A., Tomlins, T.E., Raithby, J., et al. (eds), *Statutes of the Realm*, 11 vols, vols I–IV, London, 1810–28.
17. Onslow, Fulk. Journal of Commons' Proceedings, 1572. *Historical Manuscripts Commission Reports*. The manuscripts of the House of Lords, vol. xi, *addenda*, 1514–1714, Her Majesty's Stationery Office, 1962.

18   Robinson, Richard. *A briefe collection of the queenes majesties most high and honourable courtes of recordes*, Rickard, R.L. (ed.), Camden Miscellany, XX, 3rd series, lxxxiii, Royal Historical Society, 1953.

19   Smith, Sir Thomas. *De Republica Anglorum*, Dewar, M. (ed.), Cambridge, 1982.

20   Townshend, Hayward. *Historical Collections, an exact account of the last four parliaments of Queen Elizabeth*, London, 1680.

21   Vardon, T. and May, T.E. (eds), *Journals of the House of Commons*, vol. I (1547–1628), London, 1803.

SECONDARY WORKS

The following abbreviations are used:

B.I.H.R.	*Bulletin of the Institute of Historical Research*
B.J.R.L.	*Bulletin of the John Rylands Library*
E.H.R.	*English Historical Review*
H.J.	*Historical Journal*
H.L.Q.	*Huntington Library Quarterly*
J.B.S.	*Journal of British Studies*
Parl. Hist.	*Parliamentary History*
T.R.H.S.	*Transactions of the Royal Historical Society*

General

22   Dean, D. 'Revising the History of Tudor Parliaments', *H.J.*, 32, pp. 401–11, 1989.

23   Elton, G.R. 'Tudor Government: The Points of Contact. I. Parliament', *T.R.H.S.*, 5th Series, 24, pp. 183–200, 1974.

24   Elton, G.R. ' "The Body of the Whole Realm": Parliament and Representation in Medieval and Tudor England', in *Studies in Tudor and Stuart Politics and Government. Papers and Reviews, 1946–1972*, vol. 2, pp. 19–61, Cambridge, 1974.

25   Elton, G.R. 'Studying the History of Parliament', in *Studies in Tudor and Stuart Politics and Government. Papers and Reviews, 1946–1972*, vol. 2, pp. 3–18, Cambridge, 1974.

26   Elton, G.R. 'Parliament in the Sixteenth Century: Functions and Fortunes', *H.J.*, 22, pp. 255–78, 1979.

27   Elton, G.R. 'The English Parliament of the Sixteenth Century: Estates and Statutes', in Cosgrove, A. and McGuire, J.I. (eds), *Parliament and Community*, pp. 69–95, Dublin, 1983.

28   Elton, G.R. 'The State: Government and Politics under Elizabeth and James', in Andrews, J.F. (ed.), *William Shakespeare. His World. His Work. His Influence*, 3 vols, New York, 1985, vol. 1, pp. 1–19.

29   Elton, G.R. 'Lex Terrae Victrix: The Triumph of Parliamentary Law in the Sixteenth Century', in Dean, D.M. and Jones, N.L. (eds), *The Parliaments of Elizabethan England*, pp. 15–36, Oxford, 1990.

30   Graves, M.A.R. and Silcock, R.H. *Revolution, Reaction and the Triumph of Conservatism. English History, 1558–1700*, Auckland, 1984.

31   Graves, M.A.R. *The Tudor Parliaments. Crown, Lords and Commons, 1485–1603*, London, 1985.

32   Guy, J. *Tudor England*, Oxford, 1988.

33   Lehmberg, S.E. 'The Role of Parliament in Early Modern England – a Reconsideration', in Stjernquist, N., *The Swedish Riksdag in an International Perspective* (Riksbanken Jubileumsfond), pp. 75–87, Stockholm, 1989.

34   Loach, J. *Parliament under the Tudors*, Oxford, 1991.

35   Pollard, A.F. *The Evolution of Parliament*, 2nd edn, London, 1964.

36   Roskell, J.S. 'Perspectives in English Parliamentary History', *B.J.R.L.*, 46, pp. 448–75, 1964.

37   Russell, C. 'Parliamentary History in Perspective, 1604–1629', *History*, 61, pp. 1–22, 1976.

38   Williams, P. *The Tudor Regime*, Oxford, 1979.

Fifteenth Century and Early Tudor Background

39   Bernard, G.W. *War, Taxation and Rebellion in Early Tudor England*, Brighton, 1986.

40   Bindoff, S.T. (ed.), *The House of Commons, 1509–1558*, 3 vols, *The History of Parliament*, London, 1982.

41   Chrimes, S.B. *Henry VII*, London, 1972.

42   Davies, R.G. and Denton, J.H. (eds), *The English Parliament in the Middle Ages*, Philadelphia, 1981.

43   Elton, G.R. *Reform and Reformation. England 1509–1558*, London, 1977.

44   Elton, G.R. 'Taxation for War and Peace in Early Tudor England'; in Elton, G.R., *Studies in Tudor and Stuart Politics and Government*, vol. 3, pp. 216–33, Cambridge, 1983.

45   Fox, A. and Guy, J. *Reassessing the Henrician Age: Humanism, Politics and Reform, 1500–1550*, Oxford, 1986.

46   Graves, M.A.R. 'The House of Lords and the Politics of Opposition, April–May 1554', in Wood, G.A. and O'Connor, P.S. (eds), *W.P. Morrell: A Tribute*, pp. 1–20, Dunedin, 1973.

47   Graves, M.A.R. 'The Mid-Tudor House of Lords: Forgotten Member of the Parliamentary Trinity', in McGregor, F. and Wright, N. (eds), *European History and its Historians*, pp. 23–31, Adelaide, 1977.

48   Graves, M.A.R. *The House of Lords in the Parliaments of Edward VI and Mary I. An Institutional Study*, Cambridge, 1981.

49 Graves, M.A.R. *Early Tudor Parliaments, 1485–1558*, London, 1990.

50 Lander, J.R. *Government and Community. England 1450–1509*, London, 1980.

51 Lehmberg, S.E. *The Reformation Parliament, 1529–1536*, Cambridge, 1970.

52 Lehmberg, S.E. *The Later Parliaments of Henry VIII, 1536–1547*, Cambridge, 1977.

53 Loach, J. 'Conservatism and Consent in Parliament, 1547–59', in Loach, J. and Tittler, R. (eds), *The Mid-Tudor Polity, c. 1540–1560*, pp. 9–28, London, 1980.

54 Loach, J. 'A "New Air"?', in Coleman, C. and Starkey, D. (eds), *Revolution Reassessed*, pp. 117–34, Oxford, 1986.

55 Loach, J. *Parliament and the Crown in the Reign of Mary Tudor*, Oxford, 1986.

56 Loades, D.M. *The Reign of Mary Tudor*, 2nd edn, London, 1991.

57 Loades, D.M. *The mid-Tudor Crisis, 1545–1565*, London, 1992.

58 Miller, H. 'Lords and Commons: Relations between the two Houses of Parliament, 1509–1558', *Parl. Hist.*, 1, pp. 13–24, 1982.

59 Scarisbrick, J.J. *Henry VIII*, London, 1968.

60 Storey, R.L. *The Reign of Henry VII*, London, 1968.

61 Wilkinson, B. *The Constitutional History of England in the Fifteenth Century*, London, 1964.

62 Wolffe, B.P. *Yorkist and Early Tudor Government 1461–1509*, Historical Association (Aids for Teachers Series No. 12), London, 1966.

Elizabethan Parliaments: General

63 Croft, P. 'English Parliaments Re-considered', *Parliaments, Estates and Representation*, 13 (1), pp. 75–81, June 1993.

64 Dean, D.M. and Jones, N.L. (eds), *The Parliaments of Elizabethan England*, Oxford, 1990.

65 Elton, G.R. 'Parliament', in Haigh, C. (ed.), *The Reign of Elizabeth I*, pp. 79–100, London, 1984.

66 Elton, G.R. *The Parliament of England, 1559–1581*, Cambridge, 1986.

67 Elton, G.R. 'Elizabethan Parliaments', *Early Modern History*, I, pp. 2–6, 1991.

68 Hartley, T.E. *Elizabeth's Parliaments: Queen, Lords and Commons, 1559–1601*, Manchester, 1992.

69 Jones, N.L. 'Parliament and the Governance of Elizabethan England', *Albion*, 19, pp. 327–46, 1987.

70 MacCaffrey, W.T. 'Parliament: The Elizabethan Experience', in Guth, D.J. and McKenna, J.W. (eds), *Tudor Rule and Revolution*, pp. 127–47, Cambridge, 1982.

71 Neale, J.E. *The Elizabethan House of Commons*, London, 1949.

72 Neale, J.E. *Elizabeth I and Her Parliaments*, 2 vols, London, 1953–7.
73 Notestein, W. *The Winning of the Initiative by the House of Commons*, Proceedings of the British Academy, xi, London, 1924.

Elizabethan Parliaments: Membership, Privileges, Procedures and Records

74 Dean, D.M. 'Image and Ritual in the Tudor Parliaments', in Hoak, D. (ed.), *Tudor Political Culture*, pp. 243–71, Cambridge, 1995.
75 Elton, G.R. 'The Early Journals of the House of Lords', *E.H.R.*, 89, pp. 481–512, 1974.
76 Elton, G.R. 'The Sessional Printing of Statutes, 1484 to 1547', in Ives, E.W., Knecht, R.J. and Scarisbrick, J.J. (eds), *Wealth and Power in Tudor England*, pp. 68–86, London, 1978.
77 Elton, G.R. 'The Rolls of Parliament, 1449–1547', *H.J.*, 22, pp. 1–29, 1979.
78 Graves, M.A.R. 'Freedom of Peers from Arrest: The Case of Henry, Second Lord Cromwell, 1571–1572', *American Journal of Legal History*, 21, pp. 1–14, 1977.
79 Hasler, P.W. *The House of Commons, 1558–1603*, 3 vols, The *History of Parliament*, London, 1981.
80 Jones, J. Gwynfor. *Wales and the Tudor State. Government, Religious Change and the Social Order, 1534–1603*, pp. 209–216, Cardiff, 1989.
81 Keeler, M.F. 'The Emergence of Standing Committees for Privileges and Returns', *Parl. Hist.*, 1, pp. 25–46, 1982.
82 Lambert S. 'The Clerks and Records of the House of Commons, 1600–1640', *B.I.H.R.*, 43, pp. 215–31, 1970.
83 Lambert, S. 'Procedure in the House of Commons in the Early Stuart Period', *E.H.R.*, 95, pp. 753–81, 1980.
84 Munden, R.C. ' "All the Privy Council being members of this House." A Note on the Constitutional Significance of Procedure in the House of Commons, 1589–1614', *Parl. Hist.*, 12 (2), pp. 115–25, 1993.
85 Neale, J.E. 'The Commons' Journals of the Tudor Period', *T.R.H.S.*, 4th Series, 3, pp. 136–70, 1920.
86 Pollard, A.F. 'The Clerical Organisation of Parliament', *E.H.R.*, 57, pp. 31–58, 1942.
87 Pollard, A.F. 'Receivers of Petitions and Clerks of Parliament', *E.H.R.*, 57, pp. 202–26, 1942.
88 Pollard, A.F. 'The Clerk of the Crown', *E.H.R.*, 57, pp. 312–33, 1942.

The Politics of Parliaments

89 Alsop, J.D. 'Reinterpreting the Elizabethan Commons: the

Parliamentary Session of 1566', *J.B.S.*, 29, pp. 216–40, 1990.

90 Collinson, P. *The Elizabethan Puritan Movement*, London, 1967.

91 Collinson, P. 'The Monarchical Republic of Queen Elizabeth', *B.J.R.L.*, 69, pp. 394–424, 1987.

92 Croft, P. 'Parliament, Purveyance and the City of London, 1589–1608', *Parl. Hist.*, 4, pp. 9–34, 1985.

93 Dean, D.M. 'Parliament, Privy Council, and Local Politics in Elizabethan England: The Yarmouth–Lowestoft Fishing Dispute', *Albion*, 22, pp. 39–64, 1990.

94 Elton, G.R. 'Arthur Hall, Lord Burghley and the Antiquity of Parliament', in Lloyd Jones, H., Pearl, V. and Worden, B. (eds), *History and Imagination*, pp. 88–103, London, 1981.

95 Elton, G.R. 'Piscatorial Politics in the Early Parliaments of Elizabeth I', in McKendrick, N. and Outhwaite, R.B. (eds), *Business Life and Public Policy. Essays in Honour of D.C. Coleman*, pp. 1–20, Cambridge, 1986.

96 Graves, M.A.R. 'Thomas Norton the Parliament Man: An Elizabethan MP, 1559–1581', *H.J.*, 23, pp. 17–35, 1980.

97 Graves, M.A.R. *Thomas Norton. The Parliament Man*, Oxford, 1994.

98 Heisch, Alison. 'Lord Burghley, Speaker Puckering, and the Editing of HEH Ellesmere MS 1191', *H.L.Q.*, 51, pp. 210–26, 1988.

99 Ives, E.W. *Faction in Tudor England*, Historical Association (Appreciations in History Series No. 6), London, 1979.

100 Jones, J. Gwynfor. *Early Modern Wales, c. 1525–1640*, Macmillan British History in Perspective Series, pp. 176–92, London, 1994.

101 Jones, N.L. *Faith by Statute. Parliament and the Settlement of Religion, 1559*, Royal Historical Society (Studies in History Series No. 32), London, 1982.

102 Jones, N.L. 'An Elizabethan Bill for the Reformation of the Ecclesiastical Law', *Parl. Hist.*, 4, pp. 9–34, 1985.

103 Jones, N.L. 'The Anonymous Diarist of 1571: Alias Thomas Atkins or Robert Bowes?', *Parl. Hist.*, 8 (2), pp. 329–40, 1989.

104 Jones, N.L. 'Religion in Parliament', in Dean, D.M. and Jones, N.L. (eds), *The Parliaments of Elizabethan England*, pp. 117–38, Oxford, 1990.

105 Jones, N.L. *The Birth of the Elizabethan Age. England in the 1560s*, Oxford, 1993.

106 MacCaffrey, W. 'Parliament and Foreign Policy', in Dean, D.M. and Jones, N.L. (eds), *The Parliaments of Elizabethan England*, pp. 65–90, Oxford, 1990.

107 MacCaffrey, W.: (a) *The Shaping of the Elizabethan Regime. Elizabethan Politics, 1558–72*, London, 1969; (b) *Queen Elizabeth and the Making of Policy, 1572–1588*, Princeton, New Jersey, 1981.

(NB Some of the works listed in this section justify inclusion in the following section too, e.g. nos 93, 95–7, 101–2, 104.)

The Business Record of Elizabethan Parliaments

108   Alsop, J.D. 'The Theory and Practice of Tudor Taxation', *E.H.R.*, 97, pp. 1–30, 1982.

109   Alsop, J.D. 'Parliament and Taxation', in Dean, D.M. and Jones, N.L. (eds), *The Parliaments of Elizabethan England*, pp. 91–116, Oxford, 1990.

110   Archer, I. 'The London Lobbies in the Later Sixteenth Century', *H.J.*, 31, pp. 17–44, 1988.

111   Bindoff, S.T. 'The Making of the Statute of Artificers', in Bindoff, S.T., Hurstfield, J. and Williams, C.H. (eds), *Elizabethan Government and Society: Essays Presented to Sir John Neale*, pp. 59–94, London, 1961.

112   Dean, D.M. 'Sir Symonds D'Ewes: Bills of "no great moment" ', *Parl. Hist.*, 3, pp. 157–78, 1984.

113   Dean, D.M. 'Enacting Clauses and Legislative Initiative, 1584–1601', *B.I.H.R.*, 57, pp. 140–8, 1984.

114   Dean, D.M. 'Public or Private? London, Leather and Legislation in Elizabethan England', *H.J.*, 31, pp. 525–48, 1988.

115   Dean, D.M. 'London Lobbies and Parliament: The Case of the Brewers and Coopers in the Parliament of 1593', *Parl. Hist.*, 8, pp. 341–65, 1989.

116   Dean, D.M. 'Parliament and Locality', in Dean, D.M. and Jones, N.L. (eds), *The Parliaments of Elizabethan England*, pp. 139–62, Oxford, 1990.

117   Dean, D.M. 'Pressure Groups and Lobbies in the Elizabethan and Early Jacobean Parliaments', *Parliaments, Estates and Representation*, 11, pp. 139–52, 1991.

118   Dean, D.M. 'Locality and Parliament: The Legislative Activities of Devon's MPs during the Reign of Elizabeth', in Gray, T., Rowe, M. and Erskine, A. (eds), *Tudor and Stuart Devon: The Common Estate and Government*, pp.75–95, Exeter, 1992.

119   Elton, G.R. 'Enacting Clauses and Legislative Initiative, 1559–81', *B.I.H.R.*, 53, pp. 183–91, 1980.

120   Fairclough, K. 'A Tudor Canal Scheme for the River Lea', *London Journal*, 5, pp. 218–27, 1979.

121   Fairclough, K. 'A Successful Elizabethan Project: the River Lea Improvement Scheme', *Journal of Transport History*, 3rd Series, 11, pp. 54–65, 1990.

122   Hoyle, R.W. 'Crown, Parliament and Taxation in Sixteenth-Century England', *E.H.R.*, 109, pp. 1174–96, 1994.

123   Lidington, D.R. 'Parliament and the Enforcement of the Penal Statutes: The History of the Act "In restraint of common promoters" ' (18 Eliz. 1, c. 5), *Parl. Hist.*, 8, pp. 309–28, 1989.

124   Miller, H. 'Subsidy Assessments of the Peerage in the Sixteenth Century', *B.I.H.R.*, 28, pp. 15–34, 1955.

125   Roberts, P. 'Elizabethan Players and Minstrels and the Legislation of 1572 against Retainers and Vagabonds', in Fletcher, A. and Roberts, P. (eds), *Religion, Culture and Society in Early Modern Britain. Essays in Honour of Patrick Collinson*, pp. 29–55, Cambridge, 1994.

126   Schofield, R. 'Taxation and the Political Limits of the Tudor State', in Cross, C., Loades, D.M. and Scarisbrick, J.J. (eds), *Law and Government under the Tudors. Essays Presented to Sir Geoffrey Elton*, pp. 227–56, Cambridge, 1988.

127   Tittler, R. 'Elizabethan Towns and the "Points of Contact": Parliament', *Parl. Hist.*, 8, pp. 275–88, 1989.

128   Ward, L. 'The Treason Act of 1563: A Study of the Enforcement of Anti-Catholic Legislation', *Parl. Hist.*, 8, pp. 289–308, 1989.

Parliamentary Management, Patrons and Clients, and Men of Business

129   Adams, S. 'The Dudley Clientele and the House of Commons, 1559–1586', *Parl. Hist.*, 8 (2), pp. 216–39, 1989.

130   Alsop, J.D. 'Exchequer Office-holders in the House of Commons, 1559–1601', *Parl. Hist.*, 8 (2), pp. 240–74, 1989.

131   Collinson, P. 'Puritans, Men of Business and Elizabethan Parliaments', *Parl. Hist.*, 7 (2), pp. 187–211, 1988.

132   Dean, D.M. 'Patrons, Clients and Conferences: The Workings of Bicamerism in the Sixteenth Century English Parliament', in Blom, H.W., Blockmans, W.P. and de Shapper, H. (eds), *Bicameralism: The Two Chamber System, Past and Present*, pp. 209–27, The Hague, 1992.

133   Graves, M.A.R. 'The Management of the Elizabethan House of Commons: The Council's "Men of Business" ', *Parl. Hist.*, 2, pp. 11–38, 1983.

134   Graves, M.A.R. 'Patrons and Clients: Their Role in 16th Century Parliamentary Politicking and Legislation', *Turnbull Library Record*, 18, pp. 69–85, Wellington, New Zealand, 1985.

135   Graves, M.A.R. 'The Common Lawyers and the Privy Council's Parliamentary Men-of-Business, 1584–1601', *Parl. Hist.*, 8 (2), pp. 189–215, 1989.

136   Graves, M.A.R. 'Managing Elizabethan Parliaments', in Dean, D.M. and Jones, N.L. (eds), *The Parliaments of Elizabethan England*, pp. 37–63, Oxford, 1990.

137   Loades, D. 'Politics and the "Men-of-Business" in the Tudor Parliaments', *Parl. Hist.*, 12 (1), pp. 73–7, 1993.

INDEX